IGNITE YOUR PASSION

IGNITE YOUR PASSION

Project Management Basics

Dorcas M. T. Cox

authorHOUSE®

AuthorHouse™
1663 Liberty Drive
Bloomington, IN 47403
www.authorhouse.com
Phone: 1-800-839-8640

First published by AuthorHouse   06/01/2011

ISBN: 978-1-4634-0824-4 (sc)
ISBN: 978-1-4634-0823-7 (dj)
ISBN: 978-1-4634-0822-0 (ebk)

Library of Congress Control Number: 2011909250

Printed in the United States of America

CONTENTS

To my mother, my sister, and my son, as well as all others who dare to believe and have the courage to try.

Preface

Live Your Life with a Sense of Purpose

Project management is a discipline that gives you the tools that you need to ignite your passion and live your life with a sense of purpose. Clarity of focus and purpose allows you to approach whatever you do from a meaningful perspective.

You should always use a structured approach when completing the smallest to the most elaborate initiatives. One way to realize your potential is to approach processes using a proven approach that will produce valuable results every time.

Dream big, make a plan, work hard, follow up, and celebrate are likened to the five process areas of project management. Be mindful of the risks that you may encounter along the way; they may vary based on the nature of your project. Risks may include unrealistic expectations, inadequate funding, delay in decisions, and destructive behavior exhibited by those who may be included in the process.

Despite the challenges and risks that are inherent in every situation, there are ways that you may overcome and realize success. Make sure that you have buy-in and clear benefits, put a sustainable system in place, use an approved plan to implement your initiative, and remember to have fun along the way. Role modeling the project management discipline and corresponding behaviors will add substance to your life and move you steadily toward creating a life of meaningfulness, purpose, and passion.

Introduction

Ignite Your Passion is a textbook that is included as a part of a learning program. This textbook and corresponding learning program is intended to teach you the discipline of project management in a simple and enjoyable way.

Who Should Read This Book

Ignite Your Passion is intended to appeal to learners from diverse backgrounds, experience levels, education, age, specific skills, and prior experience. As such, this book is intended to captivate the interest of the following audiences:

- high school and secondary school students.
- persons new to the field of project management.
- persons with a passion in life who want to learn how to create successful projects that help them realize their potential.

This practical learning program uses creative ways to present content that is realistic and sequential to the way that project management activities are completed in formal and informal settings.

Description of Learning Program

The learning program that this book is a part of is divided into five courses including nineteen lessons. Additional features of the learning program may be accessed via the Be a Superstar website, www.beasuperstar. org, and include:

- simulation and real-world case samples.
- information on project management knowledge and skills.

- sample-populated project templates.
- sample blank project templates.
- repository of project successes.
- rewards and recognition opportunities for learners.
- lesson plans and reference material for teachers, educators, and parents who are home schooling children.

Instructional Strategies

This learning program uses a blended learning approach inclusive of instructor-led activities, self-paced activities, field/practical experience, and job aid. The following methods are used in different places and times in the learning program:

- demonstration.
- discussion.
- question and answer exercises.
- case study involving extensive practice of new skills to solve a problem.
- classification and discrimination of new concepts.
- application of the respective templates used in project management.

In some instances, the facilitator or the self-paced learner will be directed to learning content, exercises, and activities from sources outside of the *Ignite Your Passion* book.

Media

The *Ignite Your Passion* book is developed in a way that gives the facilitator or the self-paced learner the option of skipping from one chapter or lesson in the book to the next in an eclectic way. Alternatively, facilitators or self-paced learners may opt to progress through the book by reading according to the sequential presentation of the chapters. This learning program includes a variety of media as follows:

- *Ignite Your Passion*, project management basics textbook.

- Podcasts accessed via the Be a Superstar website, www. beasuperstar.org.
- online social networking, blogs, wikis, and online chats accessed via the Be a Superstar website, www.beasuperstar.org.
- instructor-led face-to-face exchange.

These presentation methods appeal to a variety of learning styles and facilitate just-in-time learning when a quick solution to a situation, a quick reference, or a job aid is required.

Learning Assessment

This learning program is designed in a way that provides clear instructions on how to work with a real-world case scenario. Learners are directed to the Be a Superstar website, www.beasuperstar.org, via instructions found in the *Ignite Your Passion* book. These instructions, found throughout the book, allow learners to apply their knowledge and skill in the project management discipline in practical ways. At the end of the learning program, learners are encouraged to present their projects to a panel of judges (which they will organize). These judges will assess the quality of the respective project, the delivery, and the project team's ability to articulate what they did to arrive at the respective project outcome.

This learning program is not intended to teach you all details of project management. It provides a solid start in learning the skills and knowledge required to transfer into

- improved performance in class.
- improved performance at work.
- quality community-based projects.
- improved extracurricular project-related activities.
- preparation to embrace global opportunities in the twenty-first century.

Given the increasing focus on the need for enhanced efficiencies and cost-effectiveness, bringing a project in on time, in scope, and within budget is of increasing importance to organizations and individuals.

Ignite Your Passion is included as a part of a practical learning program that provides you with the expertise to realize your full potential.

Chapter 1

Dream Big

Lesson 1: Projects, Programs, and Portfolios

After studying this lesson, you should be able to:

- define a project.
- explain how projects come about.
- describe a program.
- explain how programs are managed.
- define portfolios.
- explain what is included as a part of portfolio management.
- differentiate between projects, programs, and portfolios.

An Idea

Imagine this: you get an idea, a really, really big idea for a project that you believe might just work. This project is in an area that you are passionate about. It could be in any industry, music, construction, small business, the creative arts . . . anything. Your project idea may have come about as a result of market demand, strategic opportunity, business need, customer request, technological advance, or even a legal requirement. Maybe your idea is to create a product that can either be a component of another item or an end in itself. Your project idea may be to perform a service or result, such as to produce a video, a concert, or an event.

Definition of a Project

So now what? What do you do next? Should you start planning the project? Maybe, but before you do, it may not be a bad idea to first figure out whether your idea actually fits the definition of a project. What exactly is a project? A project may be defined as any initiative that has a clear start date and a clear finish date, is intended to produce a unique product, service, or result, and is developed in greater detail as the work progresses.

Immediately you may see how your idea satisfies two of the three requirements according to the definition. Your idea may have a clear start and finish date and may be developed in greater detail as the work progresses. But what about the unique product, service, or result? What is meant by *unique*? *Unique* in this context does not mean that the methods, models, and principles used to produce your outcome are *unique*. These methods and principles may be standard in your profession or industry and are in place to govern the production of certain works.

Just because a standard method is used does not mean that you will not produce a unique outcome. For example, just because you use the principles of floral designing, which is a standard method used to design and develop floral arrangements, does not mean that the wedding contract that you will produce the floral arrangements for is not unique. That said, take a look at the components of your idea again to make sure that they satisfy the three requirements according to the definition of a project.

Programs

Now that you've determined that your project idea satisfies the definition of a project, you need to decide whether your project should be managed as a stand-alone project or whether it should be included as a part of a program or a portfolio. Your decision in this regard depends on the nature of your initiative. The terms *program* or *portfolio* are used to describe how projects are grouped based on similarities and differences. A program, for example, groups related projects together for enhanced efficiency.

Perhaps you are considering constructing a shopping center that has a number of attached and detached buildings. The construction of each building may be defined as a separate project. If managing the construction of each of these separate but related projects is achieved more efficiently and effectively by using the same techniques in a coordinated fashion, we would refer to this as a program.

Program Management

Programs are managed in a coordinated way. This allows you to gain access to benefits and control that may have been unavailable to you if each of the projects in the program were managed individually.

Portfolios

A portfolio, on the other hand, is a collection of projects or programs that are not necessarily similar. For example, a portfolio may include a home improvement project, an account cleanup project, an office renovation project, and a systems upgrade project.

Portfolio Management

Portfolio management focuses on making sure that projects and programs are reviewed so that resources can be allocated and prioritized. Another important aspect of portfolio management is the focus on making sure that projects included in the portfolio are managed in a way that is in keeping with the organization's strategies.

Key Points to Remember

- A project may be defined as any initiative that has a clear start date and clear finish date that produces a unique product, service, or result and is developed in greater detail as the work progresses.

- Just because a standard method is used does not mean that you will not produce a unique outcome.
- *Program* and *portfolio* are terms that are used to describe how projects are grouped based on similarities and differences.
- Program management allows you to gain access to benefits and control that may have been unavailable to you if each of the projects in the program were managed individually.
- A portfolio is a collection of projects or programs that are not necessarily similar.
- Portfolio management focuses on making sure that projects and programs are reviewed to prioritize resource allocation.

Discussion Questions

1. What is a project?
2. Why do projects come about?
3. How can projects be used for personal and community development?
4. What are some examples of project ideas for personal and community development?
5. What is a program?
6. What is a portfolio?
7. Why are projects, programs, and portfolios managed differently?

Debrief Questions

1. What are the key learning points?
2. What information was new to you?
3. Which concepts will you apply in the future? When?
4. What challenges do you anticipate that may limit your ability to apply the concepts?
5. What needs to be in place to overcome these challenges?
6. Who would you recommend these concepts to and why?

Activity

The following is an activity that may be completed individually or as a small group activity to assess your comprehension:

1. Answer the discussion questions above based on the material presented in this lesson.
2. Answer the debrief questions.

Lesson 2: Project Management

After studying this lesson, you should be able to:

- define project management.
- explain the five process groups that projects are categorized in.
- describe the project phases.
- differentiate between project process groups and project phases.
- state the nine knowledge areas that are included as a part of project management.

What Is Project Management

Let's say you're having lunch one day, and a colleague says to you that he or she is considering a career move into the area of project management. Before he makes his mind up, he really needs you to give him an idea of what project management involves. Naturally, you clear your mouth of food before responding; while this act has nothing to do with the definition of project management, it would be considered the polite thing to do.

There is silence. You speak, and this is what you say: "Project management includes the planning and control required to measure, analyze, forecast and report cost, and schedule performance data for decision making." Broken down, what you really should have said is that whenever there is a project, your goal should be to create a plan with the kind of structure in place that allows you to measure how you are doing for time, figure how much money you have spent, and make predictions for the future outcome of the initiative. In a nutshell, this is essentially what project management is all about. Project management is a discipline that is based on efficiency, measurement, and effective results.

When, as a project manager, you apply the knowledge, skills, tools, and techniques associated with the discipline, you are able to build a high-performance team that achieves multiple benefits, which include:

- Service excellence through efficient output and effective use of resources.
- Increase in quality and reduction of waste using performance metrics and other methods of accountability.
- Innovation in process that may contribute to achieving a competitive edge.

Knowledge Areas

You should have knowledge in a wide range of areas to complete project work from start to finish.

- First, you should identify and define the project work as well as understand how all aspects of the project work are coordinated. This knowledge requirement is referred to as project integration.
- Second, you should know how to properly determine exactly how big the project is and what it will require from start to finish. This is referred to as knowledge of scope.
- Next, you should know how to determine the cost of the project to budget and ensure that there are sufficient funds available to the project from start to finish.
- You also need to know how to properly determine and manage the schedule. This is referred to as time management.
- It is important to have knowledge of how to determine and manage quality throughout the project, as well as how to properly communicate and manage human resources, risk, and procurement.

In all, there are nine interconnected knowledge areas that you may use multiple times when managing a project from start to finish.

In addition to the need to know a whole lot of stuff, as project manager you should also have and demonstrate certain skills to effectively execute your project work. These skills include, but are not limited to, communication, budgeting, conflict management, negotiating, influencing, leadership, team building, and motivating skills.

Project Process Groups

I believe that I mentioned earlier that project management is very organized—well, maybe I didn't. Now is a good time to tell you that project management is a very organized discipline. Project activities are typically grouped into five distinct categories that represent how project work should be completed from start to finish. These categories, which are sometimes referred to as process groups, are called initiation, planning, executing, monitoring and controlling, and closing.

Project Phases

Not only are projects organized into categories but they may also be organized into phases. Organizing project work to be completed in phases allows for easier management, planning, and control of the work. Phase completion is often marked by specific, tangible outputs or multiple outputs that may be measured or easily proved. These outputs are often referred to as deliverables. Deliverables must be produced, reviewed, and approved to bring the phase or project to completion.

Project phases may be sequential, where one phase must finish before the next phase can begin; overlapping, where one phase starts before the prior phase is completed; or iterative, which means that the work for the subsequent phases is planned as the work for the previous phase is performed. The processes of initiating, planning, executing, monitoring and controlling, and closing are typically performed during each project phase. When all of the phases that a project progresses through are looked at holistically, this is referred to as the project life cycle.

Key Points to Remember

- Project management is a discipline that is based on efficiency, measurement, and effective results.
- Knowledge in a wide range of areas is required to complete the project work from start to finish.
- There are nine interconnected knowledge areas that you may use multiple times when managing a project from start to finish.
- Project work is typically organized into five different categories.
- Project work is often completed in phases.
- Project phases may be sequential, overlapping, or iterative.
- When all of the phases that a project progresses through are looked at holistically, this is referred to as the project life cycle.

Discussion Questions

1. What is project management?
2. Why is it necessary?
3. What are the five process groups?
4. Why are the five process groups necessary?
5. How are the five process groups used to manage projects?
6. How many types of phases of a project are there?
7. How do project process groups and phases interact?
8. What are the project management knowledge areas?
9. How many project management knowledge areas are there?
10. Why are knowledge areas required for managing projects?
11. How do knowledge areas interact with the five process groups?
12. What happens if the project management knowledge areas and process groups do not interact as intended?

Debrief Questions

1. What are the key learning points?
2. What information was new to you?

3. Which concepts will you apply in the future? When?
4. What challenges do you anticipate that may limit your ability to apply the concepts?
5. What needs to be in place to overcome these challenges?
6. Who would you recommend these concepts to and why?

Activity

The following is an activity that may be completed individually or as a small group activity to assess your comprehension:

1. Answer the discussion questions above based on the material presented in this lesson.
2. Answer the debrief questions.

Lesson 3: The Project Manager

After studying this lesson, you should be able to:

- state the role of the project manager.
- discuss the importance of a project manager.
- explain what a project manager needs to know and what behavioral skills he or she should demonstrate.
- demonstrate the behavior that a project manager must exhibit.
- summarize how a project manager applies knowledge and skills in and out of project settings.

The Role of the Project Manager

When you think about the role of the project manager, the first thing that comes to mind should not be going up to receive the PEMMY award for the role of lead actor in a project management drama or for role of best supporting actress in a project suspense thriller. Before you start getting too excited, calm down. This is not what we will be discussing in this lesson. At the same time, there are roles, a set of connected behaviors, and obligations that you should demonstrate in certain situations as project manager.

As project manager, you will often be required to play multiple roles. You may be a guide, an influencer, a consensus builder, an observer, a peacemaker, a taskmaster, an empathetic listener, an encourager, or a documenter based on the situation.

Guide

As a guide, you must know the steps in the process from beginning to end and carefully guide your project team, customers, and stakeholders through each phase in the project life cycle.

Influencer

As an influencer, you must ignite enthusiasm in your team and stakeholder group as you establish momentum for your project and keep the team on pace.

Consensus Builder

As a consensus builder, you must find ways to establish an environment conducive for building consensus.

Observer

In your role of observer, you must watch carefully for potential signs of strain, frustration, and resistance from members of the stakeholder group and your project team.

Peacemaker

As a peacemaker, you must move quickly to effectively restore order and direct your team toward constructive resolution when conflict arises.

Taskmaster

You are ultimately responsible for keeping your project team on track and managing the respective processes on the project.

Empathetic Listener

You must listen with empathy to understand the meaning of and relate to what is being said.

Encourager

You must praise effort and achievement at every opportunity.

Documenter

You must keep accurate records and ensure that the project management methods meet conventional standards.

It All Comes Down to Leadership

Your mission as project manager, should you choose to accept it, is essentially a call to leadership. As project manager, you may be responsible for millions of dollars in resources.

Project managers must clearly understand the project outcome and the people responsible for doing the work. Project managers who understand people communicate effectively, influence what others think, and facilitate healthy conflict resolution. This requires active listening and empathizing with and acknowledging the viewpoints of others, even those with opposing points of view.

Project leadership means knowing how and when you should establish limits and boundaries, being straightforward when communicating the message, and checking in to make sure that the message is accurately received and clearly understood. Strong leadership skills means being open to giving and receiving clear and constructive feedback that is well-timed and authentic.

A strong team leader must also be a team player. This means complementing the styles of others, valuing others, and empowering the team while building consensus.

Project success requires taking the necessary action with steady, persistent effort to build a team based on trust, where members are valued, understood, respected, and challenged to strive to achieve their very best. At the end of the day, project success all comes down to leadership.

Knowing the Lay of the Land

Knowing where the dead bodies lie in an organization may sometimes be referred to as institutional knowledge. This includes knowledge of existing organizational structure, personnel policies, technical, interpersonal, and political factors, and failed attempts in the past. You must consider all of this when you are planning and managing a project. Information regarding the way people, teams, and organizational units behave and effective use of this information may shorten the amount of time, cost, and effort you need to create and manage a high-performance team.

Skills like networking, relationship building, influencing, and team leadership are critical when identifying and documenting project roles and responsibilities and directing and managing the project team.

Efficient and effective communication plays a critical role in the success of a project. Effective communication means that information is provided in the right format, at the right time, and with the right impact. Efficient communication means providing only the information that is needed. Improper communication may delay a message delivery, communicate sensitive information to the wrong audience, or prevent information from reaching some of the required stakeholders.

Listening actively and effectively, questioning and probing ideas and situations to ensure better understanding, and resolving conflict to prevent disruptive impacts are among the skills that, when you demonstrate them effectively, may contribute to overall project success.

Key Points to Remember

- The project manager may play the role of a guide, an influencer, a consensus builder, an observer, a peacemaker, a taskmaster, an empathetic listener, an encourager, or a documenter.
- Success or failure on a project all comes down to leadership.
- A project manager should understand people, communicate effectively, influence what others think, and facilitate healthy conflict resolution.
- Knowledge of existing organizational structure, personnel policies, and technical, interpersonal, and political factors must be considered when you are planning and managing a project.
- Skills like networking, relationship building, influencing, and team leadership are critical when identifying and documenting project roles.
- Active listening and effectively questioning and probing ideas and situations are important skills that a project manager should demonstrate.

Discussion Questions

1. Who is a project manager?
2. Why is a project manager important?
3. Is a project manager really necessary?
4. What would happen if we did not have a project manager on a project?
5. How would this impact the project and its objectives?
6. What knowledge and skill does a project manager need to have?
7. What behavior does a project manager need to demonstrate?
8. How does a project manager apply knowledge and skills in and out of project settings?

Debrief Questions

1. What are the key learning points?
2. What information was new to you?
3. Which concepts will you apply in the future? When?
4. What challenges do you anticipate that may limit your ability to apply the concepts?
5. What needs to be in place to overcome these challenges?
6. Who would you recommend these concepts to and why?

Activity

The following is an activity that may be completed individually. There is also a group component in the form of a role play to assess your comprehension:

1. Answer the discussion questions above based on the material presented in this lesson.
2. Answer the debrief questions.
3. Participate in a full group role play, where the instructor will play the role of coach and each learner will play the role of project manager. The group will be given a scenario and instructions that will explain the requirements and rules of the role-play activity. Instructions for the role play will be found on the Be a Superstar website, www.beasuperstar.org.

Lesson 4: Initiate Your Project

After studying this lesson, you should be able to:

- define project initiation.
- explain the importance of project initiation.
- list and describe the steps to be taken as a part of project initiation.
- define stakeholders.
- describe the importance of stakeholders.
- explain what happens if some of the steps in project initiation are left out.
- complete templates for the documents produced as an outcome of project initiation.

Authorize a Project to Begin

You're sitting down, relaxing, and freeing your mind when you come up with another one of those ideas. Yeah, that's right, one of those ideas that look like a winner. Right off the bat, you get the urge to jump right in and go at it hard as you always do: leap from idea conception, gallop to project execution, stall, and then stop.

Resist behaving impulsively. Remember that the first step is to initiate the project. Initiating requires that you slow your thoughts down, put pen to paper, and start thinking through what it is you believe will be your greatest contribution to the world. Can you describe what you plan to produce as a result of this project? If you cannot, you may want to look at your concept again because if you cannot capture the essence of your concept in words, it is unlikely that you will be convincing anyone to get on board that train with you.

Two Things that Must Be Done

Remember, initiating officially authorizes a project, assigns a project manager, identifies the project stakeholders, and obtains your organization's commitment to the project. In addition, your project's scope and objectives are also determined in the project initiation process. That said, there are two things that you must do to properly initiate a project:

1. Create the project charter document to authorize the work of the project.
2. Identify the stakeholders to allow you to create the stakeholder register and the stakeholder management strategy documents.

Develop the Project Charter

Let's begin with the project charter—the purpose of the project charter, the importance of the project charter, and what information you should include in a project charter.

The project charter is the document that authorizes the project or the next phase of a project and also authorizes the project manager to apply resources to the project. Given the significance of the document, it is most important that you prepare the project charter correctly. Some of the source documents you may use to prepare the project charter include the project statement of work, a business case, a contract, and consideration for the internal and external environment in which the project will operate.

When a Contract Is Necessary

It may not be necessary for you to obtain input from all of these documents in order to prepare the charter document. For example, a contract may only be necessary when the organization that you are working for is performing a project for a customer outside of the organization. In this case, the kind of information that you may obtain from the contract that is necessary for inclusion in the charter may be the conditions under which the project will be executed, the time frame, and a description of the work.

When a Statement of Work Is Necessary

Sometimes a contract is not available or is not necessary because the work is being performed internal to the organization. In this case, a project statement of work is a document that you should use to obtain information such as a description of the product, service, or result that the project is undertaken to complete, the business need, the product scope description, and even the strategic plan.

Knowledge of Project Integration

You will need knowledge of project integration management when writing the project charter. This is because the project charter serves as a source document that provides information to the project management plan, the project scope statement, the stakeholder register, the requirements documentation, the requirements management plan, and the requirements traceability matrix. Some of these documents we will discuss later on when we discuss project planning.

Internal and External Environment Considerations

It is crucial that you consider the external and internal environment that the project will operate in when documenting the project charter. The areas that you should review include, but are not limited to, the organizational culture, government or industry standards, the political climate, and the organization's policies, procedures, or guidelines for conducting work.

Identify Stakeholders

The second thing that you must do to initiate a project is identify the stakeholders to obtain the information necessary to produce the stakeholder register and the stakeholder management strategy documents.

Stakeholders are people or organizations that have a vested interest in the outcome of the project or have something to either gain or lose as a result of the project. Stakeholders have the ability to influence project results.

Stakeholder Register

The stakeholder register is the document that you use to identify those people and organizations impacted by the project and document relevant information about each stakeholder. Relevant information may include name, role, position in the organization, role in the project, contact information, list of major requirements, expectations, and potential influence on the project.

Strategy to Manage Stakeholders

The stakeholder management strategy documents stakeholders and their influence on the project and analyzes the impact that they may have on the project. The stakeholder management strategy also provides a place for you to document potential strategies to increase the stakeholder's positive influence and minimize potential disruptive influence on the project.

The project charter, procurement documents, information about the company's culture, and maybe even the stakeholder register from a previous project are all possible sources from which you may obtain the necessary information.

The Importance of Communication

In order to obtain information about and communicate information to stakeholders, it is important that you have knowledge of project communication management. Project communication management is the area of project management that ensures that all of the project information (including the project plans, risk assessments, and meeting notes) is collected, documented, archived, and disposed of at the proper time.

In addition to the knowledge of communication management, it is also necessary that you demonstrate expert judgment as well as the ability to accurately analyze stakeholders. The ability to properly analyze stakeholders is a technique that entails identifying stakeholders, identifying their potential impact on the project, and assessing how stakeholders are likely to react to given situations.

Key Points to Remember

- Initiating a project officially authorizes a project, assigns a project manager, identifies the project stakeholders, and obtains the organization's commitment to the project.
- Initiating a project includes creating a project charter document and identifying stakeholders.
- A contract may only be necessary when the organization that you are working for is performing a project for a customer outside of the organization.
- A statement of work may be used when a contract is not available or is not necessary because the work being performed is internal to the organization.
- Knowledge of project integration is required when writing the project charter.
- Stakeholders are people or organizations that have a vested interest in the outcome of the project.
- The stakeholder register is the document that is used to identify those people and organizations impacted by the project.
- The stakeholder management strategy documents stakeholders and their influence on the project.
- It is important that the project manager knows how to analyze stakeholders.
- The project manager should also demonstrate skill in communication.

Discussion Questions

1. What is meant by project initiation?
2. Why is project initiation important?
3. Who are considered as stakeholders?
4. Why are stakeholders important?
5. What steps are completed as a part of project initiation?
6. What happens if some of the steps included as a part of project initiation are missed?
7. What documents are produced as a part of project initiation?
8. Who is responsible for producing project initiation documents?
9. What happens if important information is left out of project initiation documents?
10. What does it mean when project initiation documents are signed? What happens next?

Debrief Questions

1. What are the key learning points?
2. What information was new to you?
3. Which concepts will you apply in the future? When?
4. What challenges do you anticipate that may limit your ability to apply the concepts?
5. What needs to be in place to overcome these challenges?
6. Who would you recommend these concepts to and why?

Activity

The following is an activity that may be completed in project teams:
1. Answer the discussion questions.
2. Answer the debrief questions.
3. Complete the respective templates. Use social networking tools such as blogs and online chats (via the Be a Superstar website, www.beasuperstar.org) to clarify issues and continue discussion that will assist with completing the assignment.

Chapter 2

Make a Plan

Lesson 1: Plan Your Project

After studying this lesson, you should be able to:

- list and describe seventeen steps to planning a project.
- explain the purpose of subsidiary plans.
- list some subsidiary plans that may be included as a part of a project plan.
- explain the purpose of a baseline.
- cite some examples of project baselines.
- describe what is meant by the performance baseline.
- identify the kind of information that goes into the project charter.
- discuss why it is important to have a project charter.

Planning a Project

You made it out of initiation, and you are on to planning the project. Now what? No use looking dumbfounded like a deer in the headlights. Project planning is not rocket science. Just like anything else, simplify the process, follow the steps, and you're on your way to success. There are just some basic things that you have to do to plan a project.

Seventeen Steps to Planning a Project

1. Figure out what you need or want as an outcome.
2. Categorize and prioritize your requirements.
3. Plan how to manage your requirements.
4. Understand what is included in or excluded from the project.
5. Break down all of the project work into work packages.
6. List all activities in each work package.
7. Sequence all activities in each work package.
8. Figure out what resources you need to complete each activity.
9. Determine how long it will take to do the work of each activity.
10. Schedule time to complete each activity.
11. Estimate how much it will cost to complete each scheduled activity.
12. Determine your budget.
13. Outline a plan to make sure you have a quality product.
14. Assign the people to complete each activity.
15. Plan what, when, and how to communicate and to whom.
16. Plan how to identify, evaluate, and deal with risks.
17. Figure out what you need to make or buy to pull off the project.

The project management plan gives you instructions for how the project will be executed, monitored and controlled, and closed. While your project management plan itself may only be a two-page document, the fact that you may need to include a number of subsidiary plans may result in your project folder being a three-ring binder. Your goal would be to make sure that the project plan and all subsidiary plans are integrated in a coordinated fashion.

Examples of Subsidiary Plans

There is no rule that says that you must include all of these subsidiary plans in every project; that would be quite ridiculous, as some projects are so small that including a slew of subsidiary plans would be overkill.

In cases where the nature of your project dictates, you may consider including any or all of the subsidiary plans listed below. Each of these plans may be detailed based on the requirements and nature of your specific project. These subsidiary plans may include, but are not limited to:

- Requirements management plan.
- Scope management plan.
- Schedule management plan.
- Cost management plan.
- Quality management plan.
- Process improvement plan.
- Human resources plan.
- Communication management plan.
- Risk management plan.
- Procurement management plan.

Project Baselines

If you are into sports, then the term *baseline* may already be familiar to you. In baseball, the baseline is the areas within which a player must keep when running between bases. In tennis, the baseline is the back line at each end of the court. In project management, the baseline serves essentially the same purpose as it does in sports: it is the line that serves as the basis for comparison or control. It is the standard.

Once you baseline the project management plan, you can only make changes when a change request is generated and approved through the integrated change control process that is included as a part of project execution. Examples of project baselines include, but are not limited to:

- Schedule baseline.
- Cost performance baseline.
- Scope baseline.

Often the scope, schedule, and cost baseline will be combined into a performance measurement baseline that is used as an overall project baseline against which integrated performance may be measured.

Information That Goes into the Project Plan

You should really write a project charter for every project, even if the charter is only a two-paragraph document. You will find that writing a charter serves the purpose of giving your project some structure because it helps you to think through the rationale behind your project in sufficient detail to capture the essence in writing. In addition to all of that, you need the project charter to provide you with the detail that you need to start writing your project plan. Where would you get information like the project purpose or justification, project objectives, high-level requirements, project description, risks, summary milestone schedule, and summary budget if you did not write a project charter?

The project charter documents the business need, the current understanding of the customer's needs, and the new product, service, or result that the project is intended to satisfy. You need this information along with information about the organizations involved in the project that may be used to influence the project's success as well as factors that relate to the internal and external environments that surround or influence the project's success.

Key Points to Remember

- A project management plan is the document that governs the way the project will be managed.
- The project management plan is inclusive of several subsidiary plans.
- Subsidiary plans provide greater detail around how certain processes should be carried out.
- The project management plan must always be current and reflect the most recent updates.
- Information from the project charter is used when creating a project plan.

- It is very important to write a project charter when initiating a project.
- Scope, schedule, and cost baselines are combined into a performance measurement baseline.
- The performance measurement baseline is the overall project baseline against which integrated performance may be determined.

Discussion Questions

1. Why do you need steps to follow when planning a project?
2. How many steps are included in the project planning process?
3. What are the steps to take when planning a project?
4. Who is responsible for completing these steps or making sure that these steps are completed?
5. Why is it important to complete these steps?
6. Should these steps be followed sequentially or randomly? Why?
7. What happens if these steps are not completed properly or are missed completely?
8. What is the benefit of completing these steps?
9. Why is a project charter important as it relates to the project plan?
10. What is meant by the baseline?
11. What are some examples of baselines that may be used in project management?
12. What is meant by the project performance baseline?

Debrief Questions

1. What are the key learning points?
2. What information was new to you?
3. Which concepts will you apply in the future? When?
4. What challenges do you anticipate that may limit your ability to apply the concepts?
5. What needs to be in place to overcome these challenges?
6. Who would you recommend these concepts to and why?

Activity

The following is an activity that may be completed individually or as a small group:

1. Answer the discussion questions above based on the material presented in this lesson.
2. Answer the debrief questions.

Lesson 2: Scope Out Your Project

After studying this lesson, you should be able to:

- explain the importance of collecting requirements.
- list and describe ways to collect requirements.
- categorize and prioritize your requirements.
- determine how to manage your requirements.
- describe what is included in or excluded from the project.
- explain the steps in creating the Work Breakdown Structure (WBS).
- complete templates for the documents produced as an outcome of scoping your project.

Figure Out What You Need or Want as an Outcome

Right off the bat, you have to know where you are going, so that at the very least you can recognize if you are there or not. The first thing you need to do to kick off your project planning process is to figure out what it is you need or want as an outcome of the project. In other words, collect requirements.

Think about the outcome or outcomes that your project will produce at the end of the day. Often these are outcomes you could touch and feel, although sometimes the outcome may be a service. Describe what specific conditions these outcomes must have in place for you to know that your project is a success. Another way of going about this is to determine and prioritize the wants, needs, and expectations of all of the people or organizations that have a stake in your project.

Write out all of these requirements. Do not rely on your memory and walk around with all of this information in your head. We may have all experienced at some time or another how something made perfect sense in our head, and it is not until we got to writing it down that the gaping holes appeared.

Write Down All Requirements

Take the time to write down all requirements in enough detail that you, or anyone else for that matter, can measure these requirements once the project work begins. You can use a few different techniques to get requirement information from the customer. You may use interviews, questionnaires, surveys, or even observation. You may even have some other techniques of your own that may work in your situation. It does not matter which technique or combination of techniques you use to get this information from customers, as long as at the end of the day, you establish the exact requirements of all stakeholders so that the project will result in you producing the goods or service that meet their needs.

Categorize and Prioritize Your Requirements

Sometimes you may find it easy to group the requirements you need to meet the project and product objectives into categories. Some categories that have been used in the past are: quality, performance, safety, security, technical, training, support, and maintenance, to name a few.

In addition to identifying, categorizing, and prioritizing requirements, it is also useful to list the stakeholder associated with the requirements and write a couple of words that you believe capture what these stakeholders see as the mark of acceptance. It makes good sense to think this process through early on in the planning. You may come to see later that having this information is a great tool when making trade-off decisions among requirements and in managing stakeholder expectations.

Plan How to Manage Your Requirements

It is important that you have a plan to manage requirements throughout your project. This is another one of those plans that you cannot just make up, keep in your head, and not tell anybody about. Just because you have to write down a plan does not mean that you have to come up with something fancy. Something simple will do. Make sure that you include the following:

- Technique you plan to use to collect the requirements.
- Categories that will be used to group the requirements.
- Approach that you will use to prioritize the requirements.
- Attributes that you will use to trace the requirements.
- Procedure needed to change the requirements.
- Process for determining the impact of the change.
- Different methods that will be used to verify the requirements.

Defining Scope

Taking the time to collect your requirements is time well spent. You may not realize it, but what you have essentially done is begun the process of scoping your project. When you look at defining scope, you should be developing a common understanding of what is included in or excluded from your project. Scope is collectively the product, service, or result of the project.

Product scope refers to the product (features and characteristics that describe the product, service, or result of the project). Project scope describes the project management work.

The process of defining the product or project scope begins with a review of the project objectives. Objectives describe what you are trying to accomplish or produce as a result of the project. Objectives should be quantifiable and may include schedule, cost, quality, or business measures.

This information may be obtained from any documents or information that you can get your hands on that outline the project requirements or any other standard policies or guidelines.

Methods Used to Define Scope

There are several tools and techniques that you may use to define the project scope. These include looking at ways to convert the product description and project objectives into tangible outcomes. Sometimes you may need to look at several alternatives. Brainstorming and thinking outside of the box are ways that may be used to identify different ways to accomplish the project work.

Scope Statement

The scope definition process results in the creation of the scope statement. The purpose of the scope statement is to document the project objectives, tangible outcomes, and work required to produce these tangible outcomes. You may use this document to direct the project team's work and serve as a basis for future decisions.

The project scope statement serves as an agreement between the project and the customer. This agreement states precisely what the work of the project will produce. This document serves as a baseline for the project and tells everyone concerned with the project exactly what they will get when the project work is complete.

Information Included in the Scope Statement

The scope statement includes the product scope description, the product acceptance criteria, and project outcomes, exclusions, constraints, and assumptions. An exclusion is anything that is not included as a deliverable or work of the project. Be sure to note project exclusions in the project scope statement so that they can be used to manage stakeholder expectations throughout the project. Constraints are anything that either restricts the actions of the project team or dictates the actions of the project team.

Constraints

Constraints that may be encountered on a project include time, budget, scope, quality, resources, and so on. Assumptions for the purpose of project management are things that you believe to be true. The purpose for identifying, documenting, and updating assumptions in project management is so that they may be validated and so that contingency plans may be created. Information to add to the list of assumptions may be sourced from stakeholders and brainstorming exercises with the project team as well as from vendors or suppliers.

The Power of the Work Breakdown Structure

The next step is to create the work breakdown structure, or WBS. The WBS clearly describes the project's deliverables and scope. The WBS defines and organizes the project work. It assists you as well as the project leaders, participants, and stakeholders in developing a clear vision of the project's end products or outcomes.

The WBS divides the project scope into manageable packages of work, which also provides support for focusing communication with stakeholders. It assists you in clearly identifying accountability to a level of detail necessary for effectively managing and controlling the project. The WBS facilitates the reporting and analyzing of project and status data, including resource allocations, cost estimates, expenditures, and performance.

The information from the project scope statement and the requirements documentation, as well as standard policies, guidelines, templates, and other requirements, are essential when creating the WBS.

Steps in Creating a WBS

1. Identify the deliverables.
2. Organize the project work and determine the WBS structure.
3. Break down the WBS components into lower-level components.
4. Assign identification codes.

5. Verify the WBS by examining the breakdown and determine whether all components are clear and complete.

100-Percent Rule

The WBS includes 100 percent of the work defined by the project scope. Collectively, all levels of the WBS roll up to the top, so that all project work is captured and no additional work is added. The WBS should not include any work that falls outside the actual scope of the project (i.e., the WBS cannot include more than 100 percent of the work). The 100-percent rule also applies at the activity level. The work represented by the activities in each work package must add up to 100 percent of the work necessary to complete the work package.

Key Points to Remember

- Write down all requirements in sufficient detail that you or anyone else can measure these requirements once the project work begins.
- Interviews, questionnaires, and survey information from customers may be used to get requirement information.
- Grouping requirements into categories may be a good idea.
- Linking stakeholders to specific requirements helps to make sure that requirements that are important to specific stakeholders are met.
- You should have a plan to manage requirements throughout your project.
- Product scope refers to the product (features and characteristics that describe the product, service, or result of the project).
- Project scope describes the project management work.
- The scope statement documents the project's objectives, tangible outcomes, and the work required to produce these tangible outcomes.
- An exclusion is anything that is not included as a deliverable or work of the project.
- Constraints are anything that either restricts the actions of the project team or dictates the actions of the project team.
- The WBS defines and organizes the project work.

- The WBS includes 100 percent of the work defined by the project scope.

Discussion Questions

1. What is meant by collecting requirements?
2. Why is collecting requirements important on a project?
3. What does the process of collecting requirements entail?
4. What are some ways that you can go about collecting requirements?
5. How do you categorize and prioritize your requirements?
6. How do you plan to manage your requirements on a project?
7. What documents are produced as a part of collecting requirements?
8. Why is it important to understand what is included in or excluded from a project?
9. What are the steps in creating a WBS?
10. What would be the benefit of breaking down all of the project work into work packages?

Debrief Questions

1. What are the key learning points?
2. What information was new to you?
3. Which concepts will you apply in the future? When?
4. What challenges do you anticipate that may limit your ability to apply the concepts?
5. What needs to be in place to overcome these challenges?
6. Who would you recommend these concepts to and why?

Activity

The following is an activity that may be completed in project teams:

1. Answer the discussion questions.
2. Answer the debrief questions.

3. Complete the respective templates. Use social networking tools such as blogs and online chats (via the Be a Superstar website, www.beasuperstar.org) to clarify issues and continue discussion that will assist with completing the assignment.

Lesson 3: Scheduling

After studying this lesson, you should be able to:

- list all activities in each work package.
- sequence all activities in each work package.
- figure out what resources are needed to complete each activity.
- determine how long it will take to do the work of each activity.
- schedule time to complete each activity.
- complete templates for the documents produced as an outcome of scheduling.

Managing Your Time in Your Project

Have you ever experienced a situation when you thought that you had so much time to spare and yet you managed to run out of time before you competed what you had set out to do? The phenomenon of lost or stolen time not only happens in our personal lives; it often occurs on our projects as well.

Time management is essential to successfully organize and manage your life, which by the way may be considered as a project. Managing time on a project requires that you know how to properly define and sequence your activities, estimate the resources required for each activity and the time that it will take to complete, and finally put all of this information together to develop a project schedule.

Defining Activities

Be sure that you support each element of the project scope by an activity or activities that will result in the completion of the work. Defining activities documents the specific activities needed to fulfill the requirements detailed in the project scope.

Each activity describes the work that must be accomplished. The description of each activity must begin with a verb and contain a unique object. You should write the description of each activity in a way that describes a specific piece of work. A single person should be responsible for performing the activity. This is not to say that multiple resources may not be required to accomplish the activity, but it does require that a single person is responsible for the performance.

Sequencing Activities

Once you define the list of activities, you must determine and record the order in which the activities will be performed. The first step to sequencing activities in logical order is to find out whether dependencies exist among the activities. You must sequence logical relationships between activities correctly if you want to develop a realistic and achievable schedule. To avoid creating artificial or incorrect activity relationships, initial activity sequencing should be determined independent of resource availability.

Four Types of Logical Relationships

1. Finish-to-start (FS).
2. Start-to-finish (SF).

3. Finish-to-finish (FF).
4. Start-to-start (SS).

Finish-to-Start Relationship

As soon as A finishes, start B. When you have finished the project charter, present it to the sponsor for sign-off. Activity B cannot start until activity A is complete. You cannot obtain sign-off on the charter until after you have finished writing it.

Start-to-Finish Relationship

When A starts, all work on B must be finished. When you start taking your medicine, you should be finished eating all of your food. The relationship ties the start of activity A to the completion of activity B.

Finish-to-Finish Relationship

As soon as B finishes, A finishes. An example of this is cooking steak and potatoes on the barbecue. This relationship is based on ending times. Both activities can start whenever they need to as long as they finish at the same time.

Start-to-Start Relationship

As soon as A starts, immediately start B. As soon as the bride starts walking down the aisle, start taking the pictures. This relationship is based on activity start times. The ending times of each activity are not related; one activity can end at a much later time than the other.

Estimating Activity Resources

All projects from the smallest to the largest require resources. The physical resources needed to complete a project include people, equipment, supplies, and materials. Estimating activity resources is concerned with determining the types and quantities of human and material resources needed for each scheduled activity. Estimating activity resources should be closely coordinated with estimating costs, as resources are typically the largest expense that you will have on any project.

Activity Duration Estimates

When you estimate activity duration, you are looking at the work effort, resources, and number of work periods needed to complete each activity. Estimating activity durations uses information on the activity scope of work, required resource types, estimated resource quantities, and resource calendars.

Activity duration estimates are quantifiable estimates expressed as the number of work periods needed to complete a scheduled activity. Work periods are usually expressed in hours or days. Large projects may express duration in weeks or months.

Activity duration estimates are expressed in work periods, and the estimates become inputs to developing the schedule. When you are estimating activity duration, make certain to include all the time that will elapse from the beginning of the activity until the work is completed. Rely on people who are most knowledgeable of the activities you are trying to estimate to help with this process.

Critical Path

The critical path is a schedule network analysis technique that is used to determine:

- The minimum total project duration.
- The earliest possible finish dates.
- The amount of schedule flexibility (or float) in the schedule network.

The critical path technique is used to determine the earliest start date, earliest finish date, latest start date, and latest finish date for each activity. Early start and finish dates are calculated by means of a forward pass using a specified start date. Late start and finish dates are determined by means of a backward pass starting from a specified completion date.

The specified completion date may be the project early finish date determined during the forward pass calculation or a target date.

Sequential Networks

You will find that this schedule network analysis technique relies on sequential networks (one activity occurs before the next, or a series of activities occur concurrently before the next series of activities begins, and so on) on a single duration estimate for each activity.

Remember, you do not consider resource availability when using the critical path method to determine the schedule durations. The critical path is generally the longest full path on the project. Any project activity with a float time, or a slack time that equals zero, is considered a critical path task. When activities with float time use up their entire float, they can become critical path tasks.

Scenario

Imagine that you are designing and developing a simple learning program for implementation within your department. To create the program, you must complete the following steps: analyze, design, develop, monitor and control, implement, and evaluate.

The activities cannot be completed in a random order. Analysis must be completed before designing can begin. While you can develop and monitor and control at the same time, you cannot evaluate before development, monitoring and controlling, and implementation are complete. Evaluation requires that all activities leading up to it are complete.

If you add up the times for all of the activities, you will not get the time required for the entire project. This is because developing and monitoring and controlling can be done in parallel. How do you find out how long the project will take? When do we start the project in order to be finished by March 8, 2011?

Requirements to Produce a Network Diagram

1. Create a list of activities to complete for the design project.
2. Sequence the activities (the order in which they must occur); determine the predecessor and successor.
3. Estimate the time required to complete each activity.

Activity Sequence and Time Estimates

Activity Identification	Activity	Dependency	Duration
A	Analyze	None	2 days
B	Design	A	20 days
C	Develop	B	10 days
D	Monitor	B	5 days
E	Implement	C,D	3 days
F	Evaluate	E	2 days

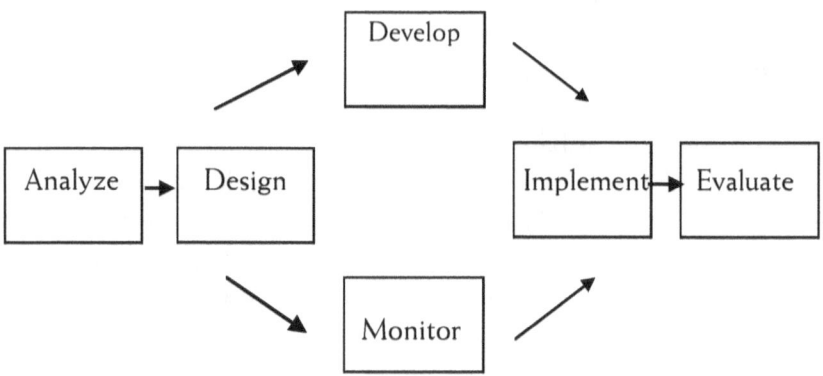

Questions

1. What does the arrow from Activity A to Activity B mean?
2. What is this dependency called? (finish-to-start, start-to-finish, finish-to-finish, or start-to-start)
3. Where do we put the dependency information on the network diagram?
4. When can Activity E start?
5. Why are there two arrows going to activity E?
6. What is the duration of the critical path?

Calculating the Earliest Finish Using a Forward Pass

If we start the analysis on the morning of January 31, 2011, when will we complete the evaluation? This is an important question, as it essentially asks "how long is our project?"

Format for Calculating Forward and Backward Passes

Earliest Start	ID	Earliest Finish
Slack	Activity Description	Slack
Latest Start	Duration	Latest Finish

Requirements to Complete a Forward Pass

1. Analysis is the first activity.
2. Fill in the "ID" field.
3. Fill in the "Activity Description" field.
4. Fill in the "Duration" field.
5. The earliest time that activity A can start is the morning of Jan 31, 2011. Fill in that field accordingly.

6. If the duration of activity A is 2 days, the earliest time that the analysis can be completed is the afternoon of February 1, 2011.
7. Put the appropriate answer in the top right-hand box as the earliest finish for activity A.
8. Repeat the same process outlined above for activities B to F.
9. The early start of an activity is the early finish of the previous activity plus one.
10. Calculate the early finish of an activity by adding its duration to the early start and subtracting one.

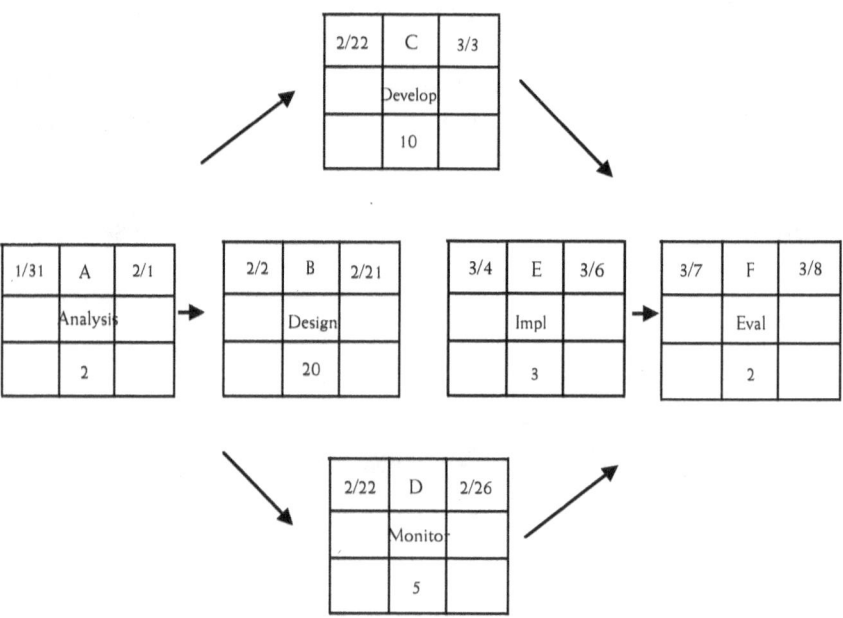

Requirements to Complete a Backward Pass

1. Begin the backward pass by making the date for the earliest and latest finish the same.
2. Calculate the late start by subtracting its duration from the late finish and adding one.
3. Move backward to the previous activity in the path. Its late finish is the late start of the previous activity minus one.

4. Calculate the late start by subtracting its duration from the late finish and adding one.

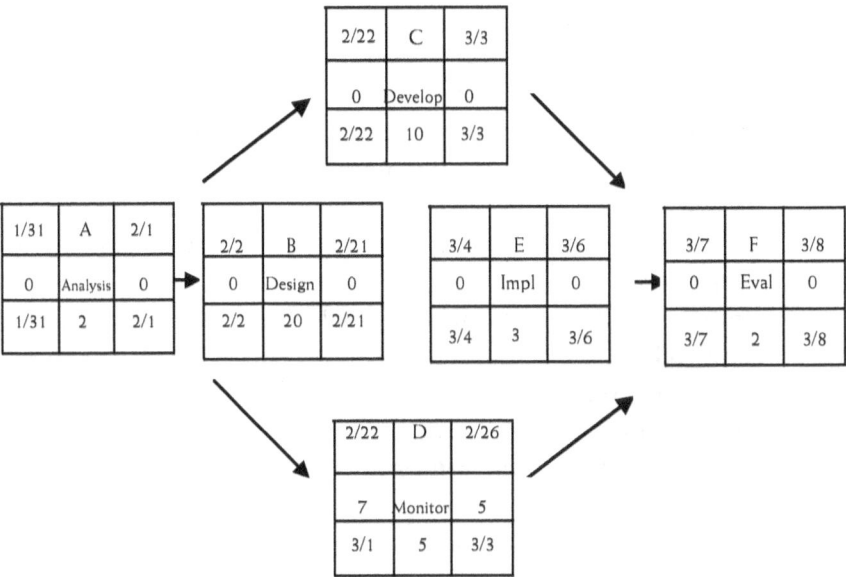

Critical Path and Slack

Calculate slack as follows:
Slack = Latest finish—Earliest finish (LF—EF).
Slack = Latest start—Earliest start (LS—ES).

Questions

1. What path is the longest path through the network diagram, or in other words, the shortest time that the project can be completed?
2. What activity does not lie on the critical path, and as such, can be delayed without affecting the project schedule?
3. Can there be more than one critical path?
4. Is this the case in this instance?

Key Points to Remember

- Support each element of the project scope by an activity or activities that will result in the completion of the work.
- Defining activities documents the specific activities needed to fulfill the requirements detailed in the project scope.
- The description of each activity should begin with a verb.
- A single person should be responsible for performing the activity.
- Once the activities are defined and listed, they should be sequenced.
- Initial activity sequencing should not include resource availability.
- The four types of logical relationships are finish-to-start, start-to-finish, start-to-start, and finish-to-finish.
- Resources are typically the largest expense on a project.
- Resources do not only include people.
- Resources may also include equipment and supplies.
- Activity duration estimates are quantifiable estimates expressed as the number of work periods needed to complete a scheduled activity.
- Work periods may be expressed in hours, days, or even months.
- The critical path technique is used to determine the earliest start date, earliest finish date, latest start date, and latest finish date for each activity.
- Any project activity with a float time or a slack time that equals zero is considered a critical path task.

Discussion Questions

1. What is meant by *activities?*
2. Why is completing all activities related to each work package on a project important?
3. What does the process of sequencing activities entail?
4. What are some ways that you can go about sequencing activities?

5. How do you determine what resources you may need to complete each activity?
6. How do you determine how long it will take to complete each activity?
7. What documents are produced as a result of scheduling?

Debrief Questions

1. What are the key learning points?
2. What information was new to you?
3. Which concepts will you apply in the future? When?
4. What challenges do you anticipate that may limit your ability to apply the concepts?
5. What needs to be in place to overcome these challenges?
6. Who would you recommend these concepts to and why?

Activity

The following is an activity that may be completed in project teams:

1. Answer the discussion questions.
2. Answer the debrief questions.
3. Complete the respective templates. Use social networking tools such as blogs and online chats (via the Be a Superstar website, www.beasuperstar.org) to clarify issues and continue discussion that will assist with completing the assignment.

Lesson 4: Let's Talk Money

After studying this lesson, you should be able to:

- estimate how much it will cost to complete each activity included as a part of a work package.
- determine the budget for the project.
- complete templates for the documents produced as an outcome of determining project costs.

Estimating Costs

Show me the money, put your money where your mouth is, money talks—these are all common ways that we express the fact that nine times out of ten, we will get to the point where we have to talk money. You know, the thing that makes the world go round or the root of all evil, depending on the way you see things.

On a project, just as in any other aspect of life where you must secure capital, you are required to develop cost estimates for all resources required for each scheduled activity. Examples of resources include labor, materials, equipment, services, facilities, inflation allowance, and contingency costs. The process of estimating costs includes weighing alternative options and examining risks and trade-offs.

Some alternatives that you may consider are make versus buy, buy versus lease, and sharing resources either across projects or departments. When estimating costs, be sure to include all costs associated with the project over its entire life cycle.

Cost estimates are usually expressed in units of some currency (e.g., dollars). Other units of measure, such as days or staff hours, may be used to facilitate comparisons, eliminating the effects of currency fluctuations.

What Goes into Estimating Costs

You may use information from a host of different areas to estimate costs. Remember those project documents that you took hours compiling? For example, the scope statement, the work breakdown structure, the work breakdown structure dictionary? Good news! The effort that you made to prepare those documents did not go to waste. Information on key deliverables, constraints, and assumptions may be necessary when estimating costs.

You may also use information from the project schedule, such as the type and quantity of resources and the amount of time that those resources are applied. These are major factors in determining costs. You may also need to look in the external environment that the project operates in to discover additional factors that may influence cost. Examples are market conditions and regional or global supply and demand conditions that may influence cost.

Where You Get This Information

There are many approaches that you may consider to obtain the information that you need to estimate cost. You can get valuable information on costs that relate to labor rates, material costs, inflation, risk factors, and other variables from the experts. Experts may often provide valuable insights about the environment and information from prior projects that are similar.

If you cannot speak with an expert, another alternative may be to review records from previous projects that are similar in scope, cost, budget, and duration to the one that you are presently working on.

Reserve Analysis

Reserve analysis (sometimes called contingency allowances) is a technique that you may use to account for cost uncertainty. You may use a percentage of the estimated cost as a contingency reserve. As more precise information about your project becomes available, you may use the contingency reserve, or you may reduce or eliminate it completely. Remember to clearly identify the contingency reserve in the cost determination.

Determine the Budget

Determining the budget requires that you add up the cost estimates of activities and establish a cost performance baseline to be used as a measurement tool for your project. Only the costs associated with your project become part of the authorized project budget. The budget will be used as a plan for allocating costs to project activities.

Key Points to Remember

- You are required to develop cost estimates for all resources required for each scheduled activity.
- Some alternatives that you may consider include make versus buy, buy versus lease, and sharing resources across projects or departments.
- Information from the scope statement, the work breakdown structure, the work breakdown structure dictionary, and the project schedule may be used when estimating costs.
- Market conditions and regional or global supply and demand conditions may also influence cost.
- Information that relates to labor rates, material costs, inflation, and risk factors is valuable data used to estimate costs.
- Reviewing records from previous projects that are similar in scope, cost, budget, and duration as the one that you are presently working on is also a good way of obtaining valuable data used to estimate costs.
- Reserve analysis is a technique that may be used to account for cost uncertainty.

- You must add up all the cost estimates of activities to determine the budget.
- The cost performance baseline is a measurement tool for your project.

Discussion Questions

1. What is meant by project costs?
2. Why is completing all activities related to each work package on a project important to determine project costs?
3. What does the process of determining project costs entail?
4. What are some ways that you can go about costing activities?
5. How do you determine what budget you may need to complete each activity?
6. What options may be available if you run out of money on a project?
7. What documents are produced as a result of project costing?

Debrief Questions

1. What are the key learning points?
2. What information was new to you?
3. Which concepts will you apply in the future? When?
4. What challenges do you anticipate that may limit your ability to apply the concepts?
5. What needs to be in place to overcome these challenges?
6. Who would you recommend these concepts to and why?

Activity

The following is an activity that may be completed in project teams:

1. Answer the discussion questions.
2. Answer the debrief questions.
3. Complete the respective templates. Use social networking tools such as blogs and online chats (via the Be a Superstar website, www.beasuperstar.org) to clarify issues and continue discussion that will assist with completing the assignment.

Lesson 5: Don't Forget Quality

After studying this lesson, you should be able to:

- state why quality is important in a project.
- describe the process for determining quality.
- explain what may happen if some steps for assuring quality are missed.
- list and describe some steps that may be followed to ensure quality.

Quality

Can you identify with a situation where you expected a particular outcome, you already had your mind geared up, your excitement and anticipation level was at an all-time high—and when the moment of truth arrived, what you thought you would get was so far removed from what you actually got that you could not believe your eyes? If you can relate to this experience, then you understand fundamentally the importance of quality.

Quality typically defines whether stakeholders' expectations are met. When you think about the process of planning quality, you should focus on targeting quality standards that are relevant to the project at hand. Your goal should be to devise a plan to meet and satisfy those standards. The quality management plan is a document that you may produce as a result of planning quality. The quality management plan describes how the quality policy will be implemented by the project management team during the course of the project. Another key output of this process is the process improvement plan. This plan documents the actions for analyzing processes to increase customer value.

Planning Quality

Identifying quality requirements or standards for your project and product are things that you must do when planning quality. This includes documenting how your project will demonstrate compliance. Quality planning should take place in conjunction with other planning processes. For example, proposed changes in the product to meet identified quality standards may require cost or schedule adjustments and a detailed risk analysis.

What Goes into Planning Quality

Remember those project documents that you took hours compiling? Great news again, your labor is not in vain. Behold the power of recycling. You get to use information in these documents in many ways again and again and for different reasons. This is why it is very important that your project documents are not only completed, but completed correctly.

You may recall that the scope statement contains the project description, major project deliverables, and acceptance criteria. Review the product scope description. It will often contain details of technical issues and other concerns that may affect quality planning. The definition of acceptance criteria may greatly increase project costs and quality costs.

Consider reviewing the stakeholder register when planning quality, as it identifies stakeholders with a particular interest in or impact on quality. The risk register is also another document that you may review when planning quality, as it includes information on threats and opportunities that may impact quality requirements. Always consider the environment. Look at government agency regulations, rules, standards, and guidelines specific to the application area and working or operating conditions of your project or product. All of these considerations may affect project quality.

Where You Get This Information

There are many approaches that you may consider to obtain the information that you need to plan quality. Consider cost-benefit analysis. Cost-benefit analysis compares the cost to produce the product, service, or result of the project to the benefit that the organization will receive as a result of executing the project. Cost-benefit analysis includes the costs to produce the product or service, the costs to take the product to market, and the ongoing operational support costs.

Consider the trade-offs of the cost of quality. It is cheaper and more efficient to prevent defects in the first place than to spend time and money fixing them later.

Cost of Quality

In preparing activity cost estimates, you may have made some assumptions about the cost of quality. The cost of quality is the total cost to produce the product or service of the project according to the quality standards. This cost includes all the work necessary to meet the product requirements, whether the work was planned or unplanned. It also includes the cost of work performed due to nonconformance to quality requirements, assessing whether the project or service meets requirements, and rework.

Prevention Costs, Appraisal Costs, and Failure Costs

Three costs associated with the cost of quality are prevention costs, appraisal costs, and failure costs. Prevention costs are the costs associated with satisfying customer requirements by producing a product without defects. These costs are manifested early in the process and include aspects such as training, design review, internal and external review, sign-off cycles, and contractor and supplier costs.

Appraisal costs are the costs that you incur to examine the product or process and make certain that the requirements are met. Appraisal costs might include costs associated with aspects such as inspections and testing.

Failure costs are what it costs when things do not go according to plan. Failure costs are also known as the cost of poor quality. Internal failure costs result when customer requirements are not satisfied while the product is still in your control. Internal failure costs may include corrective action, rework, scrapping, and downtime.

External failure costs occur when the product has reached the customer, who determines that the requirements are not met. Costs associated with external failure costs might include inspections at the customer site, returns, and customer service costs.

Quality Management Plan

The quality management plan describes how you and the project team will carry out the quality policy and documents the resources needed to carry out the quality plan. The quality management plan outlines all the processes and procedures that should be used to satisfy quality requirements, including quality control, quality assurance techniques, and continuous improvement processes. The project manager and the project staff write the quality management plan. You may assign quality actions to the activities listed on the work breakdown structure based on the quality plan requirements.

Key Points to Remember

- Quality typically defines whether stakeholder expectations were met.
- Identifying quality requirements or standards for the project and product are things that you must do when planning quality.
- Quality planning should take place in conjunction with other planning processes.
- Information on quality may be obtained from the scope statement, the stakeholder register, and the risk register.
- Government agency regulations, rules, standards, and guidelines specific to the application area and working or operating conditions of your project or product may also provide insight on quality requirements.
- Cost-benefit analysis is an approach that you may use to obtain information that you need to plan quality.
- Consider the trade-off of the cost of quality. It is cheaper and more efficient to prevent defects in the first place than to spend time and money fixing them later.
- The cost of quality is the total cost to produce the product or service of the project according to the quality standards.
- Three costs associated with the cost of quality are prevention costs, appraisal costs, and failure costs.

- Appraisal costs are the costs that you incur to examine the product or process.
- Failure costs are what it costs when things do not go according to plan.
- Internal failure costs result when customer requirements are not satisfied while the product is still in your control.
- External failure costs occur when the product has reached the customer, who determines that the requirements are not met.

Discussion Questions

1. What is meant by quality?
2. Why is it important to complete all project activities in a way that promotes quality?
3. What does the process of ensuring quality entail?
4. How can you follow the steps for ensuring quality?
5. How do you determine what quality requirements are necessary to complete each activity?
6. Who are the persons responsible for ensuring quality, and what may their respective roles in the project be?

Debrief Questions

1. What are the key learning points?
2. What information was new to you?
3. Which concepts will you apply in the future? When?
4. What challenges do you anticipate that may limit your ability to apply the concepts?
5. What needs to be in place to overcome these challenges?
6. Who would you recommend these concepts to and why?

Activity

The following is an activity that may be completed in project teams:

1. Answer the discussion questions.
2. Answer the debrief questions.

Lesson 6: Getting Good People

After studying this lesson, you should be able to:

- describe why it is important to plan for your human resources.
- explain the process for assigning the right people to complete each activity.
- summarize what may happen if there is not a plan to get people on and off of the project.
- complete templates for the documents produced as an outcome of planning human resources.

Why Develop a Human Resources Plan

Think about all of the different characteristics of the people that you work with on a regular basis. Think about their idiosyncrasies and the things that make you go "umm." If you could have anyone you wished work on your project, who would you choose? What document would you use to determine the resources that you need?

I may be able to help you with one of those answers. As project manager, you may use the activity resource requirements to determine the human resources needs. Who you choose, well, that is another conversation for another time and place. There are several things that go into developing the human resources plan for your project. These include:

- Identifying project roles and responsibilities
- Documenting project roles
- Defining the skills needed for the project

- Stating the responsibilities and required skills
- Identifying reporting relationships, and
- Creating the staffing management plan.

You should consider availability of resources, skill levels, and training needs when developing your human resources plan. These factors impact project cost, schedule, and quality and may produce risks not previously considered.

Acquiring Staff

You may ask the following questions when acquiring staff:

- Will the human resources come from within the organization or externally?
- Will team members need to work in a central location, or can they work from distant locations?
- What are costs associated with each level of expertise needed for the project?
- How much assistance can the organization's human resources department and functional managers provide to the project management team?

Staffing Management Plan

One of your goals is to produce a staffing management plan as a part of the process of developing the human resources plan. The staffing management plan describes when and how human resources requirements will be met.

Be sure to continually update your staffing management plan during the project. This plan is used to direct the process of acquiring and developing team members. Information that you should consider include acquiring staff, a resource calendar to indicate when resources are available, a staff release plan, training needs, recognition and rewards, and compliance and safety.

Key Points to Remember

- You may use the activity resource requirements to determine the human resources needs.
- You should consider availability of resources, skill levels, and training needs and then develop the human resources plan.
- The staffing management plan is produced as a part of developing the human resources plan.
- The staffing management plan must be continually updated.
- The staffing management plan describes when and how human resources requirements will be met.
- The staffing management plan provides information on staff acquisition, release, and rewards and recognition.

Discussion Questions

1. Why is it important to plan for human resources?
2. What does the process of assigning people to project activities entail?
3. Who is responsible for ensuring that human resources are assigned to the respective project activities?
4. What may happen if there is no plan to bring people on and take them off of a project?
5. What may happen to your project if the human resources are not assigned to the appropriate activity?

Debrief Questions

1. What are the key learning points?
2. What information was new to you?
3. Which concepts will you apply in the future? When?
4. What challenges do you anticipate that may limit your ability to apply the concepts?
5. What needs to be in place to overcome these challenges?
6. Who would you recommend these concepts to and why?

Activity

The following is an activity that may be completed in project teams:

1. Answer the discussion questions.
2. Answer the debrief questions.
3. Complete the respective templates. Use social networking tools such as blogs and online chats (via the Be a Superstar website, www.beasuperstar.org) to clarify issues and continue discussion that will assist with completing the assignment.

Lesson 7: Effective Communication Is Key

After studying this lesson, you should be able to:

- define a communication plan.
- explain the importance of a communication plan.
- indicate what may happen in the absence of effective communication.
- complete templates for the documents produced as an outcome of planning communications.

If Something Strange Is Happening in Your Project

If there's something strange happening in your project, what ya gonna do? Communicate! While creating a communication plan will not eliminate strange things from happening in your project, it certainly may reduce the likelihood of your project being derailed. You should include the following information when creating your communication plan:

- The communication needs of the stakeholders.
- The types of information needed.
- The format for communicating the information.
- How often the information is distributed, and who prepares it.

Your communication plan should document the approach that you will take to ensure efficient and effective communication with your stakeholders. Effective communication means that information is provided in the right format, at the right time, and with the right impact.

Efficient communication means that you provide only the information that is needed.

Improper Communication Planning

Your communication plan may represent communication across several dimensions. Examples are internal (within the project), external (with the customer, other projects, the media, the public), vertical (up and down the organization), and horizontal (with peers).

The communication methods that you present in your communication plan may be any combination of the following: formal (issuing reports, memos, briefings), informal (using e-mails, ad-hoc discussions), official (using newsletters, annual reports), or unofficial (for example, off-the-record communications). You may also choose to state whether the communications will be written, oral, verbal, or nonverbal (which includes voice inflections and body language).

Communication Skills

Communication skills that you may use on projects may include the following:

- Listening actively and effectively.
- Questioning and probing ideas and situations to ensure better understanding.
- Educating to increase the team members' knowledge so that they can be more effective.
- Fact finding to identify or confirm information.
- Setting and managing expectations.
- Persuading a person or organization to perform an action.
- Negotiating to achieve mutually acceptable agreements among parties.
- Resolving conflict to prevent disruptive impacts.
- Summarizing, recapping, and identifying the next steps.

Communication Management Plan

The communication management plan documents the types of information needs the stakeholders have, when the information should be distributed, and how the information will be delivered.

Types of Information That is Typically Communicated

- Project status.
- Project scope statement.
- Scope statement updates.
- Project baseline information.
- Risks.
- Action items.
- Performance measures.
- Deliverable acceptance.

You should determine the stakeholders' information needs as early in the planning process as possible so that, as the project team develops project planning documents, it is clear who should receive copies of them and how they should be delivered.

Information Typically Included in the Communication Management Plan

The type of information that you may present in the communication management plan will often include:

- Stakeholder communication requirements.
- Information to be communicated, including language, format, content, and level of detail.
- Reason for the distribution of that information.
- Time frame and frequency for the distribution of required information.
- Person responsible for communicating the information.
- Person responsible for authorizing release of confidential information.
- Persons or groups who will receive the information.

- Methods or technologies used to convey the information, such as memos, e-mail, or press releases.
- Resources allocated for communication activities, including time and budget.
- Escalating process identifying time frames and the management chain for escalation of issues that cannot be resolved at a lower staff level.
- Method for updating and refining the communication management plan as the project progresses and develops.
- Glossary of common terms.
- Flowcharts of the information flow in the project.
- Communication constraints, usually derived from specific legislation or regulation, technology, and organizational policies.
- Guidelines and templates for project status meetings, project team meetings, e-meetings, and e-mail.
- The use of a project website and project management software can also be included if they are used in the project.

Key Points to Remember

- Your communication plan should document the approach that you will take to ensure efficient and effective communication with your stakeholders.
- Effective communication means that information is provided in the right format at the right time and with the right impact.
- Efficient communication means that you provide only the information that is necessary.
- Your communication plan may represent communication across several dimensions.
- You may use any combination of communication methods in your communication plan.
- Listening, questioning, and negotiating are communication skills that may be commonly used on all projects.
- You should determine the communication needs of the stakeholders early in the planning process so that, as the project team develops project planning documents, it is clear

who should receive copies of them and how they should be delivered.

Discussion Questions

1. What is meant by a project communication plan?
2. Why is completing a project communication plan important?
3. What does the process of completing the project communication plan entail?
4. What would happen in the absence of effective communication?
5. What document is produced as a result of communication planning?
6. What type of information is included in the communication plan?

Debrief Questions

1. What are the key learning points?
2. What information was new to you?
3. Which concepts will you apply in the future? When?
4. What challenges do you anticipate that may limit your ability to apply the concepts?
5. What needs to be in place to overcome these challenges?
6. Who would you recommend these concepts to and why?

Activity

The following is an activity that may be completed in project teams:
1. Answer the discussion questions.
2. Answer the debrief questions.
3. Complete the respective templates in time for the next class. Use social networking tools such as blogs and online chats (via the Be a Superstar website, www.beasuperstar.org) to clarify issues and continue discussion that will assist with completing the assignment.

Lesson 8: Assess the Risk

After studying this lesson, you should be able to:

- identify risks that may present themselves in a project.
- describe some project documents that may be used to assist in identifying project risks.
- discuss the methods that may be used to identify risks in a project.
- list and describe the strategies for addressing negative risks or threats and positive risks or opportunities.
- complete templates for the document produced as an outcome of determining project risks.

Defining Risks

Risks, as they say, are ever present in our lives, and a project is no exception. "What is a risk?" you may ask. A risk is an uncertain event or condition that, if it occurs, has an effect on at least one project objective. Objectives may include scope, schedule, cost, and quality. A risk event may have one or more causes, and if it occurs, it may have one or more impacts. A cause may be a requirement, an assumption, a constraint, or a condition that creates the possibility of a positive or negative outcome.

For example, causes may include the requirement of an environmental permit to do work or having limited personnel assigned to design the project. You should apply the principles of project risk management to all projects and must include these principles in project plans and operational documents. Risk management addresses uncertainty in project estimates and assumptions. The more you know about risks and their impacts beforehand, the better equipped you are to handle a risk when it occurs.

Not all risks are bad. Risks may present future opportunities as well as future threats to the project. Known risks are the ones that you identified and analyzed, making it possible to respond promptly to those risks. Unknown risks, on the other hand, cannot be managed proactively, which suggests that you and your project team should create a contingency plan. When a risk event occurs, it ceases to become uncertain.

Planning for Risks

When you conduct your risk management planning, you are really defining how you will conduct activities to manage risk in your project. Your risk management plan assures you that the appropriate amount of resources and the appropriate time are dedicated to risk management. Planning is important to provide sufficient resources and time for risk management activities. You also need to establish an agreed-upon basis for evaluating risks. Your risk management planning process should begin as soon as your project is conceived. You should complete your risk management planning early during project planning.

Where to Look to Gather Information

As I mentioned before, you should be conscious of risks from the point of project conception. You should always be mindful of risks as you gather information to prepare project documents, some of which we have discussed before. For example, let's take a look at the project scope statement. The project scope statement provides a clear sense of the range of possibilities associated with the project and its deliverables. Your project scope statement establishes the framework for how significant your risk management effort may ultimately become.

Your project cost documents that define budgets, contingencies, and management reserves also include risk-related information that you should be mindful of. Your project schedule should include contingencies that should be reported and assessed, as should your communication plan. Your communication plan should always be clear about who will be available to share information on various risks and responses at different times and locations.

Your plan to communicate information that relates to risks should be based on your stakeholders' risk attitudes and tolerances, or the degree of risk that they are willing to accept. Risks that are threats to your project may be accepted if the risks are within tolerances and are in balance with the rewards that may be gained by taking the risks. For example, adopting a fast-track schedule is a risk taken to achieve the reward created by an earlier completion date.

Identify Risks

A risk cannot be managed unless it is first identified. After you have created a plan for managing risk, your next step should be to identify the risks. Identifying risks is an ongoing process aimed at identifying all the knowable risks to project objectives.

Your objective should be to identify risks to the maximum extent that it is practicable. At the time you identify the risk, you may also identify potential responses. As you record the possible responses, you should determine the instances where immediate action is appropriate.

Collect High-Quality Information About Risks

If you have project plans, assumptions, and historical information from previous projects, you should review these documents from the total project perspective, as well as from the perspective of individual deliverables and activity levels. Reviewing documents in this way should help you and your project team to identify risks associated with the project objectives.

You may also brainstorm and interview subject matter experts, team members, stakeholders, customers, and people with previous experience on similar projects or with specialized knowledge or industry expertise.

During these sessions, you would ask the interviewees to disclose the risks that happened on similar projects and predict what may happen on your project. Sometimes it is helpful to prompt the experts to dig deeper than the risk itself and look at the causes of the risks. This helps to define the risks more clearly and also helps later when you are developing a strategy to respond to the risk.

Risk Register

One of your goals for identifying risks is to come away with sufficient information to build a list of the risks that you identified. The risks should be described in as much detail as is reasonable in the risk register. Your goal is not only to create a list with all of the risks that you identified; you also need to have considered the root causes of those risks. You are well advised at this point to also include a list of potential responses next to the risks that you identified in the risk register. The risk register ultimately contains the outcomes of the other risk management processes as they are conducted. This results in an increase in the level and type of information contained in the risk register over time.

Strategies for Negative Risks or Threats

The four strategies that you may use for negative risks or threats are to avoid, transfer, mitigate, or accept.

Avoid

Risk avoidance involves changing the project management plan to eliminate the threat entirely. As project manager, you may choose to also isolate the project objectives from the risk's impact or change the objective that is in jeopardy. Examples of this include extending the schedule, changing the strategy, or reducing the scope.

Transfer

Risk transfer requires shifting some or all of the negative impact of a threat, along with ownership of the resources, to a third party. Transferring the risk simply gives another party responsibility for its management; it does not eliminate the risk. Transferring liability for risk is most effective when dealing with financial risk exposure. Insurance is one form of risk transfer. Contracting is another form of risk transfer. Contracting transfers specific risks to the vendor, depending on the work required by the contract. The vendor accepts the responsibility for the cost of failure. Other forms of transference that you may consider include warranties, guarantees, and performance bonds. Risk transference nearly always involves payment of a risk premium to the third party taking on the risk.

Mitigate

When you mitigate risk, you attempt to reduce the probability of a risk event and its impacts to an acceptable level. Seeing the risk ahead of time allows you to reduce the threat by planning ways around it or planning ways to reduce its impact if the risk does occur. Taking early action to reduce the probability or impact of a risk occurring on your project is often more effective than trying to repair the damage after the risk has occurred.

Examples of mitigating risks include performing more tests, using less-complicated processes, using prototypes, and using more reliable vendors.

Accept

The acceptance strategy is used when you are not able to eliminate all of the threats on your project. Acceptance of a risk event is a strategy that may be used for risks that pose either threats or opportunities to your project. Passive acceptance is a strategy that means that you won't make any plans to avoid or mitigate the risk. You are willing to accept the consequences should they occur. Passive acceptance requires no action at all other than to document the strategy, leaving the project team to deal with the risks as they occur.

Acceptance may also mean that the project team is unable to come up with an adequate response strategy and must accept the risk and its consequences. Active acceptance might mean developing contingency reserves to deal with the risks should they occur. The most common active acceptance strategy is to establish a contingency reserve, including amounts of time, money, or resources to handle the risks.

The acceptance strategy indicates that the project team has decided not to change the project management plan to deal with a risk or that they are unable to identify any other suitable response strategy.

Strategies for Positive Risks or Opportunities

Another method for planning risk responses is to consider strategies for positive risks or opportunities. The four strategies for positive risks or opportunities are to exploit, share, enhance, and accept.

Exploit

When you exploit a risk event, you are looking for opportunities for positive impacts. This is the strategy of choice when you have identified positive risks that you want to make certain will occur on your project. This strategy seeks to eliminate the uncertainty associated with a particular upside risk by ensuring that the opportunity definitely happens. An example of directly exploiting responses is assigning an organization's most talented resources to the project to reduce the time to complete or to provide lower costs than originally planned.

Share

The share strategy is similar to the transfer strategy. Here you assign the risk to a third-party owner who is best able to bring about the opportunity the risk presents. For example, perhaps your organization does great at investing but is not so good at marketing. Forming a joint venture with a marketing firm to capitalize on a positive risk will make the most of the opportunities. Other examples are risk-sharing partnerships, teams, or special purpose companies. Sharing a positive risk involves allocating some or all of the ownership of the opportunity to a third party for the benefit of the project.

Enhance

The enhance strategy closely watches the probability or impact of the risk event to assure that the organization realizes the benefits. This entails watching for and emphasizing risk triggers and identifying the root causes of the risk to help enhance impacts or probability. Examples of enhancing opportunities include adding more resources to an activity to finish early.

Accept

Accepting an opportunity is being willing to take advantage if it comes along but not actively pursuing it.

Contingent Response Strategies

A contingent response strategy is another technique that you may use when planning your risk response. Contingency planning involves planning alternatives to deal with the risks should they occur. This is different from mitigation planning in that mitigation looks to reduce the probability of the risk and its impact.

Contingency planning does not necessarily attempt to reduce the probability of the risk and its impact; contingency planning says the risk might very well occur, and you'd better have plans in place to deal with it when it does. Contingency comes into play when the risk event occurs. This implies that you need a plan for your contingencies well in advance of the threat occurring.

After you identify and quantify your risks, you should develop contingency plans and keep these plans ready. Events that trigger the contingency response include missing immediate milestones or gaining a higher priority with a supplier. Contingency allowances or reserves are a common contingency response. Contingency reserves include project funds that are held in reserve to offset any unavoidable threats to project schedule, cost, or quality. They also involve reserving time and resources to account for risks.

You should consider stakeholder risk tolerances when determining the amount of contingency reserves. Fallback plans should also be developed for risks with high impact or for risks with identified strategies that might not be the most effective at dealing with the risk.

Key Points to Remember

- A risk is an uncertain event or condition that, if it occurs, has an effect on at least one project objective.
- Project objectives may include scope, schedule, cost, and quality.
- A risk event may have one or more causes, and if it occurs, it may have one or more impacts.
- Not all risks are bad.
- Risks may present future opportunities as well as future threats to the project.
- When a risk event occurs, it ceases to become uncertain.
- When you conduct your risk management planning, you are really defining how you will conduct activities to manage risk on your project.
- Your risk management plan assures that the appropriate amount of resources and the appropriate time are dedicated to risk management.
- Your risk management planning process should begin as soon as your project is conceived.
- Risk-related information may be obtained from the project scope statement, project cost documents, project schedule, and your communication plan.
- A risk cannot be managed unless it is first identified.
- Identifying risks is an ongoing process.
- Brainstorming and interviewing subject matter experts, team members, stakeholders, customers, and people with previous experience on similar projects are great ways to collect high-quality information about risks.
- One of your goals for identifying risks is to come away with sufficient information to build a list of the risks that you identified, where the risks are described in as much detail as is reasonable.
- The four strategies that you may use for negative risks or threats are to avoid, transfer, mitigate, or accept.
- Four strategies that you may use for positive risks or opportunities are to exploit, share, enhance, and accept.

Discussion Questions

1. What is meant by project risk?
2. What impact may risk have on a project?
3. Why is it important to properly identify risks on a project?
4. What may potentially happen if you fail to properly identify risks on a project?
5. What are some ways that you can go about identifying risks on a project?
6. What are some strategies for addressing negative risks or threats?
7. What are some strategies for addressing positive risks and opportunities?
8. What is a document that is produced as a result of identifying risks in a project?

Debrief Questions

1. What are the key learning points?
2. What information was new to you?
3. Which concepts will you apply in the future? When?
4. What challenges do you anticipate that may limit your ability to apply the concepts?
5. What needs to be in place to overcome these challenges?
6. Who would you recommend these concepts to and why?

Activity

The following is an activity that may be completed in project teams:

1. Answer the discussion questions.
2. Answer the debrief questions.
3. Complete the respective templates. Use social networking tools such as blogs and online chats (via the Be a Superstar website, www.beasuperstar.org) to clarify issues and continue discussion that will assist with completing the assignment.

Lesson 9: Make or Buy

After studying this lesson, you should be able to:

- define procurements.
- give examples of when it may be necessary to procure items on a project.
- list and describe some project documents that may be used for information when determining procurement needs.
- explain some considerations that may be addressed when planning procurements.
- state the three different types of contracts that may be considered when planning procurements.

Procurement

It's late in the evening, you are on your way home from a long day at work, you are hungry, and you are tired. You have some decisions to make: do you stop at the grocery store, buy some raw ingredients, go home, slave over the stove, and wait at least another hour before you eat, or do you stop off and get some food on the go.

We make decisions on whether to purchase or acquire products, services, or results consistently throughout our everyday lives. It is no different on a project. Project procurement management includes the processes necessary to purchase or acquire products, services, or results needed from outside the project team. The organization may either be the buyer or the seller of the products, services, or result of the project.

Managing contracts and purchase orders is included as a part of procurement management. Contracts are legal documents between the buyer and the seller. Procurement contracts are legally binding and may include terms and conditions, as well as other items that the buyer specifies to establish what the seller is to perform or provide. As project manager, it is your responsibility to make certain that all procurements meet the specific needs of the project while adhering to the organization's procurement policies.

Procurement Planning

Planning your project procurement activity includes identifying potential sellers and documenting the approach and the purchase decisions as they relate to the project. When you conduct your procurement planning, you should identify those project needs that you should or must acquire products, services, or results from outside of the organization to fulfill.

When you think about whether to acquire outside support or not, you should consider what needs to be acquired, how it will be acquired, how much of it needs to be acquired, and when it should be acquired. You also need to consider who is responsible for obtaining or holding any relevant permits and professional licenses that may be required by legislation, regulation, or organizational policy in executing your project. Your project schedule requirements may significantly influence your strategy for planning procurements.

Documents That Provide Relevant Information

Scope Statement

The scope statement describes the need for the project and lists the deliverables and acceptance criteria for the product or service of the project. You should also consider assumptions that relate to the reliability of the vendor. Assuming that key resources will be available and that there will be adequate stakeholder involvement may impact the decisions that you make as they relate to planning procurements.

The product scope description that is included in the project scope statement may alert you to special considerations, such as services, technical requirements, and skills needed to produce the product of the project.

WBS and WBS Dictionary

The work breakdown structure and the work breakdown structure dictionary identify the deliverables and describe the work required for each element of the work breakdown structure.

Risk Register and Risk-Related Contract Decisions

The risk register, which includes risk-related information such as the identified risks, risk owners, and risk responses, may guide you in determining the types of services or goods needed for procurement.

Consider the risks involved with each make-or-buy decision. This information may impact the type of contract that you use with respect to mitigating risks or sometimes transferring risks to a seller. Risk-related contract decisions include agreements such as insurance, bonding services, and other items as appropriate that are prepared to specify each party's responsibility for specific risks as they relate to your procurement activity.

Activity Resource Requirements and the Project Schedule

Activity resource requirements that contain information on specific needs such as people, equipment, or location, as well as the project schedule may be used when planning procurements. The schedule contains information on time lines of mandated delivery dates. This is very important information to have when planning procurements.

Activity Cost Estimates and Cost Performance Baseline

Activity cost estimates that are developed by procurement activity are used to evaluate how reasonable the bids or proposals are that is received from potential sellers. This information works in conjunction with the cost performance baseline, which provides detail on the planned budget over time.

Requirements Documentation

You should consider requirements with contractual and legal implications, which may include health, safety, security, performance, environmental, insurance, intellectual property rights, equal employment opportunity, licenses, and permits. All of these elements should be considered when planning procurements.

Teaming Agreements

Sometimes two or more vendors may form a legal contractual agreement to work together in partnership or as a joint venture on a particular project.

If teaming agreements are used on a project, typically the scope of work requirements for competition, buyer and seller roles, and other important concerns should be predefined. Whenever the new business opportunity ends, the teaming agreement also ends.

Make-or-Buy Considerations

You should consider conducting a make-or-buy analysis when planning procurements. A make-or-buy analysis asks the question whether it is more cost-effective for a particular work to be accomplished by the project team or whether the work should be purchased from outside sources. Sometimes capacity may exist within the project organization, but it may be committed to working on other projects. In this case, the project may need to source effort from outside the organization to meet its scheduled commitments.

Costs should include both direct and indirect costs. The buy side of the analysis includes both the actual out-of-pocket costs to purchase the product, as well as the indirect costs of supporting the purchasing process and purchased item. In other words, direct costs include the actual cost to purchase the product or service and indirect costs such as ongoing maintenance costs.

Costs don't necessarily mean the cost to purchase. In make-or-buy analysis, the cost of leasing items versus the cost of buying them may also be considered.

Other considerations in make-or-buy analysis include elements such as capacity issues, skills, availability, and trade secrets. You may need strict control for a process that cannot be outsourced. Budget constraints may also influence make-or-buy decisions.

Expert Judgment

You may also consider the use of expert judgment when planning your project procurement activities. Expert judgment may also be used to develop or modify the criteria that will be used to evaluate seller proposals.

Expert judgment may involve the services of legal staff to assist with unique procurement issues, terms, and conditions. Such judgment, including business and technical expertise, may be applied to both the technical details of the acquired product, services, or results, and to various aspects of the procurement management processes.

Contract Types

You would be well advised to know the basic contract types that are commonly used when planning procurements. There are three different types of contracts included in this category:

- Fixed price.
- Cost reimbursable.
- Time and material.

Fixed Price or Lump Sum

Fixed price contracts may be disastrous for both the buyer and the seller if the scope of the project is not well defined or the scope changes dramatically. On the other hand, this type of contract may be relatively safe for both the buyer and the seller when the original scope is well defined and remains unchanged.

If you are leaning toward the use of this contract type, it is important that you have well-defined deliverables. Fixed price contracts typically reap only small profits for the seller and force the contractor to work productively and efficiently. This type of contract also minimizes cost and quality uncertainty.

Cost Reimbursable Contracts

Cost reimbursable contracts are the second type of contract included in the category of contract types. These contracts are as the name implies. The allowable costs defined in the contracts that are associated with producing the goods or services are charged to the buyer.

All the costs the seller takes on during the project are charged back to the buyer, and thus the seller is reimbursed. Cost reimbursable contracts carry the highest risk to the buyer because the total costs are uncertain. As problems arise, the buyer has to shell out even more money to correct the problems.

The advantage to the buyer with this type of contract is that scope changes are easy to make and can be made as often as you want—but it will cost you. This category of contract involves payments (i.e., cost reimbursements) to the seller for *all* legitimate actual costs incurred for completed work, *plus* a fee representing the seller's profit. Cost reimbursable contracts may also include financial incentive clauses whenever the seller exceeds or falls below defined objectives, such as costs, schedule, or technical performance targets.

Cost reimbursable contracts have lots of uncertainty associated with them. The contractor has little incentive to work efficiently or become productive. This type of contract protects the contractor's profit because increasing costs are passed to the buyer rather than taken out of profits, as would be the case with a fixed price contract. Cost reimbursable contracts are used most often when the project scope contains a lot of uncertainty, such as for cutting-edge projects and research and development. They are also used for projects that have large investments early in the project life.

Time and Material Contracts

Time and material contracts is the third and final contract type. Time and material contracts are a cross between fixed price and cost reimbursable contracts. The full amount of the material costs is not known at the time the contract is awarded.

This resembles a cost reimbursable contract because the costs will continue to grow during the contract's life and are reimbursable to the contractor. The buyer bears the biggest risk in this type of contract. The full value of the agreement and the exact quantity of the items to be delivered may not be defined by the buyer at the time of the contract award.

Time and material contracts may also increase in contract value as if they were cost reimbursable contracts. Many organizations require not-to-exceed values and time limits be placed in all time and material contracts to prevent unlimited cost growth. Time and material contracts may resemble fixed price contracts when certain parameters are specified in the contract, such as unit rates for material or labor. These rates are often preset and agreed upon by the buyer and the seller ahead of time. These rates may also include the seller's profits when both parties agree on the values for specific resource categories, such as senior engineer at specified hourly rates or categories of materials at specified rates per unit. Time and material contracts are most often used when human resources with specific skills are needed and when you can quickly and precisely define the scope of work for the project.

Key Points to Remember

- Project procurement management includes the processes necessary to purchase or acquire products, services, or results needed from outside the project team.
- The organization may either be the buyer or seller of the products, services, or result of the project.

- Contracts are legal documents between the buyer and the seller.
- Planning your procurement activity includes identifying potential sellers and documenting the approach and the purchase decisions as they relate to the project.
- When you think about whether to acquire outside support or not, you should consider what needs to be acquired, how it will be acquired, how much of it needs to be acquired, and when it should be acquired.
- You also need to consider who is responsible for obtaining or holding any relevant permits and professional licenses that may be required by legislation, regulation, or organizational policy in executing your project.
- The scope statement, the WBS, the WBS dictionary, the risk register, risk-related contract decisions, activity resource requirements, activity cost estimates, cost performance baseline, requirements documentation, teaming agreements, and project schedule are all documents that you should consult when planning your project procurement needs.
- You should consider conducting a make-or-buy analysis when planning procurement.
- You should consider the use of expert judgment when planning your project procurement activities.
- Expert judgment may involve the services of legal staff to assist with unique procurement issues, terms, and conditions.
- Fixed price or lump sum, cost reimbursable, and time and material are all examples of contract types.

Discussion Questions

1. What is meant by procurement?
2. Why are contracts and purchase orders necessary when planning the procurement requirements for the project?
3. What is included as a part of planning procurement activities?
4. What should be some considerations when determining whether or not to acquire products, services, or results from outside of the organization to meet the project requirements?

5. What are some documents that may be used to provide insight on the project procurement requirements?
6. Why should you consider conducting a make-or-buy analysis?
7. Why should you include experts when making decisions that relate to your project procurement plans?
8. Who are some of the experts that you may use when making decisions that relate to your project procurement plans?
9. What are the three contract types?
10. Which contract type may potentially reap the greatest rewards for the seller?
11. Which contract type requires a well-defined scope and deliverables?
12. What are the characteristics of a time and material contract?

Debrief Questions

1. What are the key learning points?
2. What information was new to you?
3. Which concepts will you apply in the future? When?
4. What challenges do you anticipate that may limit your ability to apply the concepts?
5. What needs to be in place to overcome these challenges?
6. Who would you recommend these concepts to and why?

Activity

The following is an activity that may be completed in project teams:

1. Answer the discussion questions.
2. Answer the debrief questions.
3. Complete the respective templates. Use social networking tools such as blogs and online chats (via the Be a Superstar website, www.beasuperstar.org) to clarify issues and continue discussion that will assist with completing the assignment.

Chapter 3

Work Hard

Lesson 1: Acquire Your Team

After studying this lesson, you should be able to:

- explain what is meant by acquiring your team.
- describe the kind of information that you may obtain from the human resources plan that may assist you in acquiring the project team.
- list and describe the events that may occur in the external environment that may impact your ability to acquire the project team.
- state the kind of information that may be obtained from within the organization that may assist with acquiring the project team.
- list and describe four methods that may be used when acquiring the project team.
- describe the importance of rewarding and recognizing the project team.

Getting the Top Picks

You are slumping over your desk, forehead cupped in both hands, reflecting on the current state of your project and thinking about how you will get the right people on your project team. You are tired of being turned down for the high-quality staff and being forced to accept the misfits. Imagine the star performers calling you and begging you to accept them as a part of your project team.

It is important that you get the right people assigned to your project team. You may acquire your project staff from inside or outside of the organization. This may come in the form of employees hired specifically for your project or as contract help. It is your job as project manager to ensure that the resources are available and skilled in the project activities to which they are assigned, although this may not always happen in practice.

What Goes into Acquiring the Project Team

Use the human resources plan as one of your primary source documents. The human resources plan should provide you with information that you may use to guide you on how your project human resources may be identified, staffed, managed, controlled, and eventually released from the project. Your human resources management plan should include information like:

- Roles and responsibilities defining the positions, skills, and competencies that the project demands.

- Project organization charts indicating the number of people needed for the project.
- Staffing management plan outlining the time period each project team member will be needed, as well as other information that is important to acquiring the project team.

Information from the External Environment

Events happening in the external environment that may influence your ability to acquire your project team include, but are not limited to:

- Existing information for human resources, including who is available, their competency levels, their prior experience, their interest in working on the project, and their cost rate.
- Human resources policies such as those that affect outsourcing.
- Organizational structure.
- Location or multiple locations.

Information from Within the Organization

Organizational processes may influence your ability to acquire your project team. These include, but are not limited to, organizational standard policies, processes, and procedures.

Methods for Acquiring the Project Team

You may use several methods for acquiring your project team. Four that are described below are preassignment, negotiation, acquisition, and virtual teams.

Preassignment

Preassignment may happen when your project is put out for bid and specific team members are promised as part of the proposal. Preassignment may also happen when internal project team members are promised and assigned as a condition of your project. When staff members are promised as part of the project proposal—particularly on internal projects—they should be identified in the project charter.

Negotiation

If you are a functional manager, you may be familiar with using the negotiation technique. This is a common technique used to ensure that the project receives appropriately competent staff in the required time frame and that the project team members will be able, willing, and authorized to work on the project until their responsibilities are completed.

The project management team may need to negotiate with other project management teams within the performing organization to appropriately assign scarce or specialized human resources. The project management team may also need to negotiate with other project management teams within the external organization, vendors, suppliers, contractors, and so on for appropriate, scarce, specialized, qualified, certified, or other human resources. Special consideration should be given to external negotiating policies, practices, processes, guidelines, and legal and other such criteria. The project management team's ability to influence others plays an important role in negotiating staff assignments, as do the politics of the organization involved.

Acquisition

Acquisition is another method that may be used to secure your project team members. When the performing organization lacks the in-house staff needed to complete a project, the requested services may be acquired from outside sources. This may involve individual consultants or subcontracting work to another organization.

Virtual Team

The availability of electronic communications such as e-mail, audio conferencing, web-based meetings, and videoconferencing has made such teams feasible. A virtual team does not necessarily work in the same location. They have little or no time spent fact-to-face, but their members all share the goals of the project and have roles to fulfill. Virtual teams allow for the inclusion of persons from different geographic locations, those who work different hours or shifts than the other team members, those with mobility limitations, and so on.

Communication planning is increasingly important in a virtual team environment. Additional time may be needed to set clear expectations, facilitate communications, develop protocols for resolving conflict, include people in decision making, and share credit in successes.

Creating the Right Environment

Project team members need the right environment, where they can feel a sense of pride in doing the work that they enjoy. A strong alignment between the basic components of the job and the employee's talents and strengths helps to create the right work environment for project team members to find internal rewards from the work itself.

Rewarding Team Members

Project team member recognition and rewards do not necessarily have to be costly. At the same time, the types of recognition and rewards that team members receive should be things that they believe justify the time, effort, and mental and emotional sacrifice that they put into their work.

Align Rewards and Recognition to Team Member Values

It is a known fact that people are different. As such, a reward or recognition that may be effective to one team member may not necessarily be effective for another. To be effective, rewards and recognition should be aligned with the project team member's values.

Align Rewards and Recognition to the Organization's Values

Rewards and recognition should not only be aligned with project team members' values but should also align to your organization's values.

Sometimes organizations capture their values in the form of mission statements, vision statements, core values, and the like. These written values are circulated among employees, customers, and the external community.

Ensure That Your Rewards and Recognition Program Is Effective

Involve your project team members as much as possible in designing and developing the rewards and recognition program that is associated with the project. Find out from your project team members what they value and, as much as possible, align rewards and recognition to these values. Reward and recognize project team members in a way that means something to them. Clearly state the reward criteria. Make the criteria known to all team members and reward and recognize every team member who meets the required criteria.

Key Points to Remember

- Use the human resources plan as one of your primary source documents when acquiring the project team.
- Your human resources plan should provide you with information that you may use to guide you on how your project human resources may be identified, staffed, managed, controlled, and eventually released from the project.
- Human resources policies, such as those that affect outsourcing, may influence your ability to acquire your project team.
- Four methods that you may use to acquire your project team include preassignment, negotiation, acquisition, and virtual teams.
- Preassignment may happen when your project is put out for bid and specific team members are promised as part of the proposal.
- Negotiation is a common technique that is used to ensure that the project receives appropriately competent staff in the required time frames and that the project team members will be able, willing, and authorized to work on the project until their responsibilities are completed.

- When the performing organization lacks the in-house staff needed to complete a project, the requested services may be acquired from outside sources.
- A virtual team does not necessarily work in the same location.
- Project team members need the right environment, where they can feel a sense of pride in doing the work that they enjoy.
- Project team member recognition and rewards do not necessarily have to be costly.
- To be effective, rewards and recognition should be aligned with the project team members' values.
- Rewards and recognition should also be aligned to the organization's values.

Discussion Questions

1. What is included as a part of acquiring the project team?
2. Why is it important to have completed the human resources plan during the planning process?
3. What information should be included as a part of the human resources plan?
4. What kind of information from the external environment may impact your ability to acquire the right staff for the project?
5. What should you do if you are unable to acquire the staff that you initially requested for the project?
6. What are the similarities and differences between techniques such as preassignment, negotiation, and acquisition that are used when acquiring the project team?
7. Why is it important to create the right kind of environment in terms of rewarding and recognizing the project team?
8. How important is it to align rewards and recognition to the individual's as well as to the organization's values?

Debrief Questions

1. What are the key learning points?
2. What information was new to you?
3. Which concepts will you apply in the future? When?

4. What challenges do you anticipate that may limit your ability to apply the concepts?
5. What needs to be in place to overcome these challenges?
6. Who would you recommend these concepts to and why?

Activity

The following is an activity that may be completed individually or as a small group:

1. Answer the discussion questions above based on the material presented in this lesson.
2. Answer the debrief questions.

Lesson 2: Distribute Information and Manage Expectations

After studying this lesson, you should be able to:

- cite the ways that information may be presented to stakeholders on a project.
- discuss some documents that may be used to assist with understanding the way information should be distributed on a project.
- list and describe some communication methods that support the process of distributing information on a project.
- explain the connection between group size and conflict-resolution techniques.
- describe the variety of ways that project information may be distributed.
- examine the six elements for inclusion in stakeholder notification.
- describe what is meant by the term *managing stakeholder expectations*.
- examine the purpose of the issues log and the change log.

Distribute Project Information

I am sure that you can relate to the feeling of being the last one to be told about an important event or situation that directly affects you. This is not a good feeling, especially if it is a situation where you may have prevented an outcome or reduced the consequences of some actions had you known about this important information in time.

Failing to make sure that you distribute the right information to the people on your project can bring your project to a screeching halt and leave you standing alone in the dirt. Distributing project information is the process of making relevant information available to project stakeholders as planned. This may come about in several ways:

- Status reports.
- Project meetings.
- Review meetings, and so on.

You are required to perform the process of distributing project information throughout the entire project life cycle and in all management processes. The focus here is mainly in the execution process, which includes implementing the communication management plan as well as responding to unexpected requests for information.

Helpful Hints

If you are wondering how to go about distributing project information, here are some helpful hints.

Remember, the communication plan tells you how the project-related information is to be distributed and the specific timing around that process. There are also performance reports.

Performance reports used to distribute project performance and status information should be made available prior to the project meetings and should be as precise and current as possible. Forecasts are updated and reissued based on work performance measurements provided as the project is executed. Information about the projects past performance may impact the project in the future. The organization's policies, procedures, and guidelines regarding information distribution may also influence the way project information is distributed. Always use templates, historical information, and lessons learned if they are available to you.

Communication Methods

Communication methods include all means feasible to communicate project information to the proper recipients, such as meetings, e-mail, videoconferences, conference calls, and so on. Every aspect of your job as a project manager will involve communication. It is estimated that a project manager spends as much as 90 percent of his or her time communicating in one form or another.

Communication skills are arguably one of the most important skills a project manager can have. Communication skills are even more important than technical skills. Good communication skills foster an open, trusting environment and are a project manager's best asset.

Information Exchange

Information exchange involves a sender, message, and receiver.

Sender
The sender is the person responsible for putting the information together in a clear and concise manner. The information should be complete and presented in a way that the receiver will be able to correctly understand. The message should be relevant to the receiver.

Message
The message is the information being sent or received. It may be written, verbal, nonverbal, formal, informal, internal, external, horizontal, or vertical. Horizontal communications are messages sent to and received from peers. Vertical communications are messages sent to and received down to subordinates and up to executive management.

Receiver
The receiver is the person for whom the message is intended. The receiver is responsible for understanding the information correctly and making sure that she has received all the information. Receivers filter the information that they receive through their knowledge of the subject, culture, influences, language, emotions, attitudes, and geographic locations. The sender should take these filters into consideration

when sending messages so that the receiver will clearly understand the message that was sent.

Methods of Information Exchange

Senders, receivers, and messages are the elements of communication. The way the sender packages or encodes the information and transmits it and the way the receiver unpacks or decodes the message are the methods of communication exchange. Senders encode messages. Encoding is a method of putting the information into a format the receiver will understand.

Language, pictures, and symbols are used to encode messages. Encoding formats the message for transmitting. Transmitting is the way the information gets from the sender to the receiver. Spoken words, written documentation, memos, e-mail, and voice mail are all transmitting methods.

Decoding is what the receiver does with the information when he gets it. He converts it into an understandable format. Usually this means that he reads the memo, listens to the speaker, reads the book, and so on.

Forms of Communication

Communication occurs primarily in written or verbal form. Verbal communication is easier and less complicated than written communication and is usually a faster method of communication. Written communication, on the other hand, is an excellent way to get across complex, detailed messages.

Detailed instructions are better provided in written form because it gives the reader the ability to go back over information that she is not sure about. Both verbal and written communication might take a formal or an informal approach.

Generally speaking, the project manager should take an informal approach when communicating with stakeholders and project team members outside of status meetings. This makes the project manager appear more open and friendly and easier to approach with questions and issues.

Group Size and Conflict Resolution

Group size makes a difference when trying to resolve a conflict or make a decision. The larger the group, the more lines of communication and the more difficult it will be to reach a decision. Groups of five to ten people have a manageable number of participants and have been shown to make the most accurate decisions. If your team and your stakeholders trust that you can communicate the vision and the project goals and report on the project status accurately and honestly, you will most likely be successful.

Information Distribution Tool

An information distribution tool is the final tool and technique required for distributing information. Project information may be distributed using a variety of tools, including:

- Hard-copy document distribution, manual filing systems, press releases, and shared-access electronic databases.
- Electronic communication and conferencing tools, such as e-mail, fax, voice mail, telephone, video and web conferencing, websites, and web publishing.
- Electronic tools for project management, such as web interfaces to scheduling and project management software, meeting and virtual office support software, portals, and collaborative work management tools.

Six Elements for Inclusion in Stakeholder Notification

The six elements that should be included as a part of distributing information to keep stakeholders informed of project activity are stakeholder notification, project reports, project presentations, project records, feedback from stakeholders, and lessons learned documentation.

Stakeholder Notification

Stakeholder notifications involve notifying the stakeholders when you have implemented solutions and approved changes, updated project status, resolved issues, and so on.

Project Reports

Project reports include project status reports and minutes from project meetings, lessons learned, closure reports, and other documents from all the process outputs throughout the project. If you are keeping an issue log, the issues would be included with the project reports as well.

Project Presentations

Project presentations involve presenting project information to the stakeholders and other appropriate parties when necessary. The presentations might be formal or informal and depend on the audience and the information being communicated.

Project Records

Project records include memos, correspondence, and other documents concerning the project. The best place to keep information like this is in a project notebook or in a set of project notebooks depending on the size of the project.

The project notebooks are ordinary three-ring binders where project information gets filed. They are managed by the project manager or project office and contain all information regarding the project. This information may also be backed up in the company intranet, on a project website, or on CDs.

Individual team members might keep their own project records as well, in notebooks or electronically. These records serve as historical information once the project is closed.

Feedback from Stakeholders

Feedback received from the stakeholders that may improve future performance on projects may be captured and documented. If the information has an impact on the current project, distribute it to the appropriate team members so that future project performance may be modified to improve results.

Lessons Learned Documentation

Lessons learned are information that you gather and document throughout the course of the project that may be used to benefit the current project, future projects, or other projects currently being performed by the organization. Lessons learned may include positive as well as negative lessons.

During the process of distributing information, you will begin conducting lessons learned meetings focusing on many different areas depending on the nature of the project. These areas might include project management processes, product development, technical processes, project team performance, stakeholder involvement, and so on.

Lessons learned meetings should always be conducted at the end of project phases and at the end of the project at a minimum. Team members, stakeholders, vendors, and others involved on the project should participate in these meetings. It is important to understand and to make team members aware that lessons learned meetings are not intended to be finger-pointing experiences. The purpose of the lessons learned meetings is to understand what went well and why, so it may be repeated for future projects, and what did not go well and why, so that it may be performed differently on future projects.

The meetings can create team-building sessions because an atmosphere of trust and sharing may be created while building on each other's strengths to improve performance. The reasons or causes for the issues or the corrective action taken should be documented, as well as any other information that future projects may benefit from.

Managing Stakeholder Expectations

Managing stakeholder expectations is the process of communicating and working with stakeholders to meet their needs and address issues as they occur.

Managing stakeholder expectations involves communication activities directed toward project stakeholders to influence their expectations, address concerns, and resolve issues.

This may include:

- Actively managing stakeholders' expectations to increase the likelihood of project acceptance.
- Addressing concerns that have not become issues yet, usually related to the anticipation of future problems.
- Uncovering and discussing concerns and assessing risks.
- Clarifying and resolving issues that have been identified.

The resolution may result in a change request or may be addressed outside of the project, for example, postponed for another project or phase or deferred to another organizational entity. Managing expectations helps to increase the probability of project success by ensuring that the stakeholders understand the project benefits and risks.

This enables stakeholders to be active supporters of the project and to help with risk assessment of project choices. By anticipating people's reactions to the project, preventive actions may be taken to win their support or minimize potential negative impacts. The project manager is responsible for managing stakeholder expectations. Actively managing stakeholder expectations decreases the risk that the project will fail to meet its goals and objectives due to unresolved stakeholder issues. It also limits disruptions during the project.

Issues Log

An issue log or action item log may be used to document and monitor the resolution of issues. It may be used to facilitate communication and ensure a common understanding of issues.

Issues do not usually rise to the importance of becoming a project or activity, but are usually addressed in order to maintain good, constructive working relationships among various stakeholders, including team members. The issues are clearly stated and categorized based on urgency and potential impact. An owner is assigned an action item for resolution, and a target date is usually established for closure. Unresolved issues may be a major source of conflict and project delays.

Change Log

A change log is used to document changes that occur during a project. These changes and their impact to the project in terms of time, cost, and risk must be communicated to the appropriate stakeholders.

Key Points to Remember

- Distributing information is the process of making relevant information available to project stakeholders as planned.
- Performance reports required to distribute project information and status information should be made available before the project meeting and should be as precise and current as possible.
- Organizational policies, procedures, and guidelines may influence the way information is distributed.
- Communication methods include all means feasible to communicate project information to the proper recipients, including meetings, e-mail, videoconferencing, conference calls, and so on.
- It is estimated that a project manager spends as much as 90 percent of his time communicating in one form or another.
- Communication skills are arguably one of the most important skills a project manager can have.

- Information exchange involves a sender, a message, and a receiver.
- The sender is the person responsible for putting the information together in a clear and concise manner.
- The message is the information being sent.
- The receiver is the person for whom the message is intended.
- Senders, receivers, and messages are the elements of communication.
- Communication occurs primarily in oral or verbal form.
- Group size makes a difference when trying to resolve a conflict or make a decision.
- Project information may be distributed using a variety of tools.
- Stakeholders should be notified when you have implemented solutions, updated project status, resolved issues, and so forth.
- Project reports include project status reports and minutes from previous meetings, lessons learned, closure reports, and other documents from all the process outputs throughout the project.
- Project presentations involve presenting project information to the stakeholders and other appropriate parties when necessary.
- Project records include memos, correspondence, and other documents concerning the project.
- Feedback received from the stakeholders that may improve future performance on projects may be captured and documented.
- Lessons learned may include positive and negative lessons
- Managing stakeholder expectations is the process of communicating and working with stakeholders to meet their needs, addressing issues as they occur.
- An issue log or action item log may be used to document and monitor the resolution of issues.
- A change log is used to document changes that occur during a project.

Discussion Questions

1. Why is it important to ensure that project information is properly distributed?

2. What is the purpose of a performance report?
3. Why may communication skills be even more important to a project manager than technical skills?
4. Why is it necessary to have more than one method of information exchange?
5. How does the size of the group make a difference when trying to resolve conflict?
6. What are some ways that project information may be distributed?
7. How can the lessons learned document be used to benefit future projects?
8. Why should managing stakeholder expectations be a concern to a project manager?
9. How can issues and changes be managed on a project?

Debrief Questions

1. What are the key learning points?
2. What information was new to you?
3. Which concepts will you apply in the future? When?
4. What challenges do you anticipate that may limit your ability to apply the concepts?
5. What needs to be in place to overcome these challenges?
6. Who would you recommend these concepts to and why?

Activity

The following is an activity that may be completed in project teams:

1. Answer the discussion questions.
2. Answer the debrief questions.
3. Complete the respective templates. Use social networking tools such as blogs and online chats (via the Be a Superstar website, www.beasuperstar.org) to clarify issues and continue discussion that will assist with completing the assignment.

Chapter 4

Follow Up

Lesson 1: Monitor and Control Your Project

After studying this lesson, you should be able to:

- explain the importance of monitoring and controlling the project.
- list and describe some activities that may be included as a part of monitoring and controlling the project.
- list and describe some results of monitoring and controlling the project.
- describe what is meant by *integrated change control*.
- explain what is meant by *verifying the scope*.
- discuss the importance of scope verification.

Monitor and Control the Project

You may be familiar with the saying that when the cat's away, the mouse takes over your entire operation. Well, that's a modified version of the saying, but I am sure you get the point. The moral is, if you leave something, or someone for that matter, too long unattended, things tend to go awry.

Monitoring and controlling the project work is the process of tracking, reviewing, and regulating the progress to meet the performance objectives defined in the project management plan. This includes measuring project performance to identify variances from the project plan and get the project back on track.

Monitoring

Monitoring includes collecting, measuring, and distributing project information, and assessing measurements and trends to effect project improvement. Continuous monitoring gives the project team insight into the health of the project and identifies any areas that may require special attention.

Controlling

Control includes determining corrective or preventive actions or replanning and following up on action plans to determine if the actions taken resolved the performance issue. The monitoring and controlling project work is concerned with:

- Comparing actual project performance against the project management plan.
- Assessing performance to determine whether any corrective or preventive actions are indicated, and then recommending those actions as necessary.
- Identifying new risks and analyzing, tracking, and monitoring existing project risks to make sure the risks are identified, their status is reported, and appropriate risk response plans are being executed.
- Maintaining an accurate, timely information base concerning the project's product(s) and their associated documentation through project completion.
- Providing information to support status reporting, progress measurement, and forecasting.
- Providing forecasts to update current cost and current schedule information.

- Monitoring implementation of approved changes as they occur.

Results of Monitoring and Controlling the Project

Change Requests

You may need to issue change requests as a result of comparing planned results to actual results. Change requests may expand, adjust, or reduce project or product scope. Changes may impact the project management plan, project documents, or product deliverables. Changes may include, but are not limited to, corrective action, preventive action, and defect repair.

Corrective Action

Corrective action is a documented direction for executing the project work to bring expected future performance of the project work in line with the project management plan.

Preventive Action

Preventive action is a documented direction to perform an activity that may reduce the probability of negative consequences associated with project risks.

Defect Repair

Defect repair is the formally documented identification of a defect in a project component, with a recommendation to either repair the defect or completely replace the component.

Updating Your Project Management Plan

Your project management plan may more than likely need updating as a result of monitoring and controlling the project work. The areas of your project management plan that you may update include, but are not limited to:

- Schedule management plan.
- Cost management plan.
- Quality management plan.
- Scope baseline.
- Schedule baseline.
- Cost performance baseline.

Updating Your Project Documents

You will also need to update some project documents as a result of your monitoring and controlling activities. The project documents that may be updated include, but are not limited to:

- Forecasts.
- Performance reports.
- Issue log.

Integrated Change Control

The integrated change control process serves as an overseer, so to speak, of the monitoring and controlling processes. This is where you establish the project's change control process. Change requests may come about during project execution. These change requests may include the need for corrective actions, preventive actions, and defect repair.

How Changes Come About

Changes may be requested by any stakeholder involved with the project. Although changes may be initiated verbally, you should insist that they are always recorded in written form and entered into the change management or configuration management system. Change requests are subject to the process specified in the change control and configuration control systems.

Those change request processes may require information on estimated time impacts and estimated cost impacts. Every documented change request must be either approved or rejected by some authority within the project management team or an external organization.

On many projects, the project manager is given authority to approve certain types of change requests as defined in the project's roles and responsibilities documentation. Sometimes, a change control board may be required to approve or reject change requests. The roles and responsibilities for these boards are clearly defined within the configuration control and change control procedures and are agreed upon by appropriate stakeholders.

Many large organizations provide for a multitiered board structure, separating responsibilities among the boards. If the project is being provided under a contract, then some proposed changes may need to be approved by the customer, as per the contract.

Why Changes Come About on Projects

Changes come about on projects for many reasons. As project manager, it is your responsibility to manage these changes and see to it that organizational policies regarding changes are implemented. Changes do not necessarily mean negative consequences. Changes may produce positive results as well.

It is important that you manage this process carefully, because too many changes—even a single significant change—will impact cost, schedule, scope, or quality. Once a change request is submitted, you have some decisions to make.

Questions to Ask Yourself Once a Change Request Is Submitted

Should the change be implemented? If so, what is the cost to the project in terms of project constraints (cost, time, scope, and quality)? Will the benefits gained by making the change increase or decrease the chances of project completion?

Things to Consider as They Relate to Change

Just because a change is requested does not mean that you have to implement it. You will always want to discover the reasons for the change to determine whether it is justifiable, and you want to know the cost of the change. Remember that cost can take the form of increased time.

When you perform integrated change control, you review all change requests, approving changes and managing changes to the deliverables. It is important that you consider the organizational policies and procedures, project documents, and project management plan during this process.

You must ensure that the project management plan, the project scope statement, and other deliverables are maintained by carefully and continuously managing changes. This is done by either rejecting changes or by approving changes, thereby assuring that only approved changes are incorporated into a revised baseline.

Some Requirements for Approved Changes

Approved change requests may require new or revised cost estimates, activity sequences, schedule dates, resource requirements, and analysis of risk-response alternatives. These changes may require adjustments to the project management plan or other project management documents.

The extent to which you apply the level of change control depends on the application area, complexity of the specific project, contract requirements, and context and environment in which the project is performed.

Change Management Activities Included in Integrated Change Control

These include:

- Influencing the factors that circumvent integrated change control so that only approved changes are implemented.
- Reviewing, analyzing, and approving change requests promptly, which is essential, as a slow decision may negatively affect time, cost, or the feasibility of a change.
- Maintaining the integrity of baselines by releasing only approved changes for incorporation into the project management plan and project documents.
- Reviewing, approving, or denying all recommended corrective and preventive actions.
- Coordinating changes across the entire project (e.g., a proposed schedule change will often affect cost, risk, quality, and staffing).
- Documenting the complete impact of change requests.

Configuration Management System

A configuration management system with integrated change control provides a standardized, effective, and efficient way to centrally manage approved changes and baselines within the project. Configuration control is focused on the specification of both the deliverables and the processes, while change control is focused on identifying, documenting, and controlling changes to the project and the product baselines.

Project-wide application of the configuration management system, including change control processes, accomplishes three main objectives. Three things that may be accomplished by applying the configuration management system are that it:

- Establishes an evolutionary method to consistently identify and request changes to established baselines, and to assess the value and effectiveness of those changes.

- Provides opportunities to continuously validate and improve the project by considering the impact of each change.
- Provides the mechanism for the project management team to consistently communicate all approved and rejected changes to the stakeholders.

Verify Project Scope

The primary purpose of verifying the scope is to formally accept completed deliverables and obtain sign-off that the deliverables are satisfactory and meet stakeholder expectations. Verifying scope includes reviewing deliverables with the customer or sponsor to ensure that they are completed satisfactorily, and obtaining formal acceptance of deliverables by the customer or sponsor.

Scope verification differs from quality control. Scope verification is primarily concerned with acceptance of the deliverables. Quality control is primarily concerned with correctness of the deliverables and meeting the quality requirements specified for the deliverables. Quality control is generally performed before the scope is verified.

Key Points to Remember

- Monitoring and controlling the project focuses on measuring project performance to identify variances from the project plan and get the project back on track.
- Monitoring the project includes collecting, measuring, and distributing project information and assessing measurements and trends to effect project improvement.
- Control includes determining corrective or preventive actions or replanning and following up on action plans to determine if the actions taken resolved the performance issue.
- A change request may be issued as a result of comparing planned results to actual results.
- Change requests may include corrective action, preventive action, and defect repair.
- Integrated change control oversees the process of monitoring and controlling the project plan.

- Changes may come about as a result of requests made by stakeholders.
- A change request should always be made in writing.
- Changes come about for many reasons.
- Approved change requests may require new or revised cost estimates, activity sequences, schedule dates, resource requirements, and analysis of risk-response alternatives.
- Coordinating changes across the entire project is included as a part of integrated change control.
- Configuration control focuses on the specification of both the deliverables and the processes.
- Change control is focused on identifying, documenting, and controlling changes to the project and the product baselines.
- Verifying scope formally accepts completed deliverables and obtains sign-off that the deliverables are satisfactory and meet the stakeholder, customer or sponsor's expectations.
- Scope verification is primarily concerned with acceptance of the deliverables.

Discussion Questions

1. What would happen if you did not monitor and control the project work?
2. What is the difference between monitoring a project and controlling the project? Why is it important that both of these are done?
3. Why do changes come about?
4. What is integrated change control?
5. How do changes come about?
6. What are some questions that you may ask yourself once a change request is submitted?
7. What things should you consider as they relate to changes on a project?
8. What are some requirements for approved changes?
9. What are some change management activities that are included as a part of performing integrated change control?
10. What is a configuration management system?
11. What does the process of verifying scope entail?

12. Why is scope verification important?

Debrief Questions

1. What are the key learning points?
2. What information was new to you?
3. Which concepts will you apply in the future? When?
4. What challenges do you anticipate that may limit your ability to apply the concepts?
5. What needs to be in place to overcome these challenges?
6. Who would you recommend these concepts to and why?

Activity

The following is an activity that may be completed in project teams:

1. Answer the discussion questions.
2. Answer the debrief questions.

Lesson 2: Control Scope, Schedule, and Costs

After studying this lesson, you should be able to:

- state what is meant by *controlling scope*.
- explain the importance of controlling scope.
- explain what is meant by *controlling the schedule*.
- describe what is included as a part of cost control.
- examine the purpose of earned value management.
- summarize what is included as a part of earned value management.

All Inclusive

Have you ever had the opportunity to go to an all-inclusive resort for a holiday? I am told that when you pay for your package, it includes room, meals, drinks, amenities, and lots of fun.

Well, project scope is essentially the same as all inclusive. Project scope describes the work that is required to produce the product, service, or result of the project. I am not sure if it happens in all projects, but sometimes I am told that having fun is also a requirement that should be included in the scope.

The broad product scope statement usually includes the product description. The product description describes the characteristics, features, and functionality of the product, service, or result.

What Is Included as a Part of Controlling Scope

The process of controlling scope involves the following:

- Monitoring the status of both the project and the product scope.
- Monitoring changes to the project and product scope.
- Monitoring work results to ensure that they match the expected outcomes.

Any modifications to the agreed-upon work breakdown structure are considered a scope change. This means that adding or deleting activities or any modifications to the existing activities on the work breakdown structure constitute a project scope change. Changes in product scope require changes to the project scope as well.

Example

Let's say that one of your project deliverables is to design a piece of specialized equipment that is integrated into your final product. Let's say that because of engineering setbacks and some miscalculations, the specialized equipment requires design modifications. The redesign of this equipment impacts the end product, or product scope.

Since changes to the product scope impact the project requirements, which are detailed in the project scope document, changes to the project scope document are also required. These changes, along with the recommended corrective actions, should be processed through the integrated change control process.

Unapproved or undocumented changes that sometimes make their way into the project are referred to as *scope creep*. Scope creep can kill an otherwise viable project. Little changes add up and eventually impact budget, schedule, and quality.

Importance of Scope Control

Scope control is the process of monitoring the status of the project and product and managing changes to the scope baseline. Controlling the project scope ensures all requested changes and recommended corrective or preventive actions are processed through the integrated change control process.

Project scope control is also used to manage the actual changes when they occur and is integrated with the other control processes. Uncontrolled changes are also referred to as scope creep. Change is inevitable, thereby mandating some type of change control process.

Summary of Scope Change

When scope changes are requested, you should investigate all areas of the project to determine what the changes will impact. Your project team should perform estimates of the impact and of the amount of time needed to make the changes.

Sometimes, the change request is so extensive that even the time to perform an estimate should be evaluated before proceeding. In other words, if the project team is busy working on estimates, they are not working on the project. Extensive change requests could impact the existing schedule because of the time and effort needed just to evaluate the change.

Cases like these require that a determination is made to ask the change control board to decide whether the change is important enough to allow the project team to work on the estimates. Always remember to update the stakeholders regarding the changes that are being implemented and their impacts. They will want to know how the changes impact the performance baselines, including the project costs, project schedule, project scope, and quality.

Schedule Control

Controlling the schedule is the process where you monitor the status of your project to update the project's progress and manage changes to the schedule baseline. This includes:

- Determining the current status of the project schedule.
- Influencing the factors that create schedule changes.

- Determining that the project schedule has changed.
- Managing the actual changes as they occur.

Performance Reviews

Performance reviews measure, compare, and analyze schedule performance, such as actual start and finish dates, percent complete, and remaining duration for work in progress. If earned value management is utilized (see more information below on this tool), the schedule variance and schedule performance index are used to assess the magnitude of schedule variances.

An important part of schedule control is to decide if the schedule variation requires corrective action. For example, a major delay on any activity not on the critical path may have little effect on the overall project schedule, while a much shorter delay on a critical or near-critical activity may require immediate action.

Performance reviews examine elements such as start and end dates for schedule activities and the time remaining to finish incomplete activities.

Variance Analysis

Variance analysis is another technique used for controlling the schedule. Schedule performance measurements (schedule variance and schedule performance index) are used to assess the magnitude of variation to the original schedule baseline.

The total float variance is also an essential planning component to evaluate project time performance. Important aspects of project schedule include determining the cause and degree of variance relative to the schedule baseline and deciding whether corrective or preventive action is required.

Controlling Costs

Controlling costs is the process of monitoring the status of the project to update the project budget and manage changes to the cost baseline. Updating the budget involves recording actual costs spent to date. Any increase to the authorized budget can only be approved through the integrated change control process.

Monitoring the expenditure of funds without regard to the value of work being accomplished for such expenditures has little value to the project, other than to allow the project team to stay within the authorized funding. Thus, much of the effort of cost control involves analyzing the relationship between the consumption of project funds and the physical work being accomplished for such expenditures.

The key to effective cost control is the management of the approved cost performance baseline and the changes to that baseline.

What Is Included in Project Costs

Project costs include:

- Influencing the factors that create change to the authorized cost baseline.
- Ensuring that all change requests are acted on in a timely manner.
- Managing the actual changes when and as they occur.
- Ensuring that cost expenditure does not exceed the authorized funding, by period and in total for the project.
- Monitoring cost performance to isolate and understand variances from the approved cost baseline.
- Monitoring work performance against funds expended.

Earned Value Management

Earned value management is one of the most effective performance measurement and feedback tools in project management. Earned value management helps to clearly see objectively where a project is and where it is going, compared to where it was supposed to be and where it was supposed to be going.

Questions that Earned Value Management Can Answer

Earned value management can play a role in answering management questions that are critical to the success of every project, such as:

- Are we ahead of or behind schedule?
- How efficiently are we in using our time?
- When is the project likely to be completed?
- Are we currently under or over budget?
- How efficiently are we using our resources?
- What is the remaining work likely to cost?
- What is the entire project likely to cost?
- How much will we be under or over budget at the end?

If the application of earned value management to a project reveals that the project is behind schedule or over budget, the project manager can use earned value management methodology to help identify:

- Where problems are occurring.
- Whether problems are critical or not.
- What it will take to get the project back on track.

As a performance management methodology, earned value management adds some critical practices to the project management process. These practices occur primarily in the areas of project planning and control and are related to the goal of measuring, analyzing, forecasting, and reporting cost and schedule performance data for evaluation and action by workers, managers, and other key stakeholders.

Key Points to Remember

- Project scope describes the work that is required to produce the product, service, or result of the project.
- The product description includes the characteristics, features, and functionality of the product, service, or result.

- Any modification to the agreed-upon work breakdown structure is considered a scope change.
- Changes to the product scope require changes to the project scope as well.
- Unapproved or undocumented changes that sometimes make their way into the project are referred to as scope creep.
- Little changes add up and eventually impact budget, schedule, and quality.
- Scope control is the process of monitoring the status of the project and product and managing changes to the scope baseline.
- When scope changes are requested, you should investigate all areas of the project to determine what the changes will impact.
- Always remember to update the stakeholders regarding the changes that are being implemented and their impacts.
- Controlling the schedule is the process of monitoring the status of your project to update the project's progress and manage changes to the schedule baseline.
- Performance reviews measure, compare, and analyze schedule performance, such as actual start and finish dates, percent complete, and remaining duration for work in progress.
- An important part of schedule control is to determine whether schedule variation requires corrective action.
- Important aspects of project control include determining the cause and degree of variance relative to the schedule baseline and deciding whether corrective or preventive action is required.
- Controlling costs is the process of monitoring the status of the project to update the project budget and manage changes to the cost baseline.
- Any increase to the authorized budget can only be approved through the integrated change control process.
- Earned value management helps to clearly see objectively where the project is and where it is going, compared to where it was supposed to be and where it was supposed to be going.

Discussion Questions

1. Why is it important to control scope on a project?
2. What is involved in controlling scope on a project?
3. What does any modification to the agreed-upon work breakdown structure be interpreted as?
4. What are uncontrolled changes in a project referred to as?
5. Why should you update the stakeholders regarding the changes that are being implemented and their impacts?
6. What is defined as *schedule control*?
7. Why are performance reviews important as they relate to schedule control?
8. What is variance analysis, and why is variance analysis used?
9. What is the key to effective cost control?
10. What are included as part of project costs?
11. What is the definition of *earned value*?
12. What kinds of questions can earned value answer?

Debrief Questions

1. What are the key learning points?
2. What information was new to you?
3. Which concepts will you apply in the future? When?
4. What challenges do you anticipate that may limit your ability to apply the concepts?
5. What needs to be in place to overcome these challenges?
6. Who would you recommend these concepts to and why?

Activity

The following is an activity that may be completed in project teams:

1. Answer the discussion questions.
2. Answer the debrief questions.

Lesson 3: Report Performance and Control Risk

After studying this lesson, you should be able to:

- discuss the documents that may be used to obtain information for reporting project performance.
- explain the importance of performance reports.
- state the importance of monitoring and controlling risks.
- explain how risks are monitored and controlled in a project.

Performance Reporting

I am sure that we can remember (some of us with trepidation) what it felt like when at the end of the school term, we had to present our parents with our report cards. We always knew that the reckoning day would come and that they would find out what we were doing (or not doing), but when the day finally arrived, there was a whole lot of sweating bullets.

Hopefully if you manage your project well, you will not need to sweat bullets. At the same time, you do need to report on the project's performance. Just as in school our performance was compared to the standard, the same holds true for a project. Project performance reporting is the process where the collection of baseline data occurs and is documented and reported. Performance reporting involves collecting information regarding project progress and project accomplishments and reporting them to stakeholders. You may also report this information to project team members, the management team, and other interested parties.

Reporting may include information concerning project quality, costs, scope, schedule, procurement, and risk. It may be presented in the form of status reports, progress measurements, or forecasts. The performance reporting process involves the periodic collection and analysis of baseline versus actual data to understand and communicate the project progress and performance, as well as to forecast the project results.

Performance reports need to provide information at an appropriate level for each audience. The format may range from simple status report to more elaborate reports. A simple status report might show performance information such as percent complete or status dashboards for each area (i.e., scope, schedule, cost, and quality). A complete report should also include forecasted project completion (including time and cost).

More Elaborate Reports May Include

- Analysis of past performance.
- Current status of risks and issues.
- Work completed during the period.
- Work to be completed next.
- Summary of changes approved in the period.
- Other relevant information that must be reviewed and discussed.

These reports may be prepared regularly or on an exception basis.

Source Data Required to Produce Performance Reports

Project Management Plan

You should review the project management plan. It provides information on project baselines. The performance measurement baseline is an approved plan for the project work to which the project execution is compared, and deviations are measured for management control. The performance measurement baseline typically integrates scope, schedule, and cost parameters of a project, but may also include technical and quality parameters.

Work Performance Information

You can use the information from project activities that is collected on performance results, such as:

- Deliverable status.

- Schedule progress.
- Cost incurred.

Work Performance Measurement

Work performance information is used to generate project activity metrics to evaluate actual progress compared to planned progress. These metrics include, but are not limited to:

- Planned versus actual schedule performance.
- Planned versus actual cost performance.
- Planned versus actual technical performance.

Budget Forecasts

You may use budget forecast information from cost control. This provides information on the additional funds that are expected to be required for the remaining work, as well as estimates for the completion of the total project work.

Organizational Procedures

Some project considerations are influenced by the internal organization that the project operates in. Some of these considerations that impact project performance reporting activities include, but are not limited to:

- Report templates.
- Policies and procedures that define the measures and indicators to be used.
- Organizationally defined variance limits.

Performance Reports

You are required to document and report project performance information to the stakeholders in the form of performance reports. This requirement should be outlined in the communication management plan. Performance reports organize and summarize the information gathered and present the results of any analysis compared to the performance measurement baseline.

Reports should provide the status and progress information, at the level of detail required by various stakeholders, as documented in the communication management plan. These reports may take many forms, including S-curves (cost baselines are recorded in this way), bar charts, tables, and histograms.

Monitor and Control Risks

Monitoring and controlling risks involves implementing response plans, tracking and monitoring identified risks, and identifying and responding to new risks as they occur. Anticipated risks that are included in the project management plan are addressed during the life cycle of the project.

You should continuously monitor the project work for new, changing, and outdated risks. The process of monitoring and controlling risks applies techniques such as variance and trend analysis, which require the use of performance information generated during project execution.

Other Purposes for Monitoring and Controlling Project Risk

Some of the other purposes that you may have for monitoring and controlling risk are to determine if the project assumptions are still valid or if the analysis showing an assessed risk has changed or can be retired. You should also be concerned whether risk management policies and procedures are being followed and whether contingency reserves of cost or schedule should be modified in alignment with the current risk assessment.

Monitoring and controlling risk may involve choosing alternative strategies, executing a contingency or fallback plan, taking corrective action, and modifying the project management plan. You should ensure that the risk response owner reports periodically to the project manager on the effectiveness of the plan, as well as on any unanticipated effects and any correction needed to handle the risk appropriately. Monitoring and controlling risks also includes updating the organizational process assets, including project lessons learned databases and risk management templates, for the benefit of future projects.

Key Points to Remember

- Project performance is the process where the collection of baseline data occurs and is documented and reported.
- You may report this information to project team members, the management team, and other interested parties.
- Reporting may include information concerning project quality, costs, scope, schedule, procurement, and risk.
- Performance reports may be presented in the form of status reports, progress measurements, or forecasts.
- Performance reports need to provide information at an appropriate level for each audience.
- The project management plan is a great source of data for performance reporting, as it provides information on project baselines.
- Information on project activities that is collected on performance results, such as deliverable status, schedule progress, and cost incurred, may be used for performance reporting.
- Work performance information is used to generate project activity metrics to evaluate progress compared to planned progress.
- You may use budget forecast information from cost control as a source of data on project performance.
- Some project considerations are influenced by the internal organization that the project operates in.
- Performance reports organize and summarize the information gathered and present the results of any analysis compared to the performance measurement baseline.
- Performance reports may take many forms.
- Monitoring and controlling risks involves implementing response plans, tracking and monitoring identified risks, and identifying and responding to new risks as they occur.

- You should continuously monitor the project work for new, changing, and outdated risks.
- Monitoring and controlling risks may involve choosing alternative strategies, executing a contingency or fallback plan, taking corrective action, and modifying the project management plan.

Discussion Questions

1. Why should you be concerned about the project's performance report?
2. What information should be included as a part of the project's performance report?
3. What formats may project performance reports take?
4. What information may be obtained from the project management plan that may be used in the project performance report?
5. Why is work performance information good to use when reporting on the project's performance?
6. What is meant by work performance measurement?
7. Where would you get budget forecast information that you may need as a part of project performance reporting?
8. What are some project considerations that are influenced by the internal organization as they relate to project performance reporting?
9. What is included as a part of monitoring and controlling risks?
10. Why should you monitor and control risks in a project?

Debrief Questions

1. What are the key learning points?
2. What information was new to you?
3. Which concepts will you apply in the future? When?
4. What challenges do you anticipate that may limit your ability to apply the concepts?
5. What needs to be in place to overcome these challenges?
6. Who would you recommend these concepts to and why?

Activity

The following is an activity that may be completed in project teams:

1. Answer the discussion questions.
2. Answer the debrief questions.

Chapter 5

Celebrate

Lesson 1: Close Your Project

After studying this lesson, you should be able to:

- explain what is meant by administering procurements.
- state why administering procurements is required as a part of closing a project.
- list and describe the two things that are required to close a project or phase.
- list and describe the four formal types of project endings.

Administer Procurements

Have you ever been to a function, and as soon as the official program was over, everyone headed for the door and acted as if they did not know that there was a closing out and cleanup process involved?

Well, it would not be so bad if you were one of the ones heading out the door; but unfortunately as a project manager, you should be the last to leave. This is particularly true if you need to sign off on some work and cut some checks for work that was completed as a part of the project and product requirements.

Administering procurements is the process of monitoring your vendors' performance and ensuring that all the requirements of the contracts are met. When multiple vendors are providing goods and services to your project, administering procurements involves coordinating the interfaces among all vendors as well as administering each of the contracts. Both the buyer and the seller must administer the procurement contract for similar purposes. Each ensures that both parties meet their contractual obligations and that their own legal rights are protected.

The process of administering procurements ensures that the seller's performance meets procurement requirements and that the buyer performs according to the terms of the legal contract. The legal nature of contractual relationships makes it imperative that the project management team is aware of the legal implications of actions taken when administering any procurement.

Administering procurements includes application of the appropriate project management processes to the contractual relationship(s) and integration of the outputs from these processes into overall management of the project. The integration will occur at multiple levels when there are multiple sellers and multiple products, services, or results involved.

The project management processes that are applied may include, but are not limited to:

- Direct and manage project execution—to authorize the seller's work at the appropriate time.
- Report performance—to monitor contract scope, cost, schedule, and technical performance.
- Perform quality control—to inspect and verify the adequacy of the seller's product.
- Perform integrated change control—to assure that changes are properly approved and that all those with a need to know are aware of such changes.
- Monitor and control risk—to ensure that risks are mitigated.

The Financial Management Component

Administering procurements also has a financial management component that involves monitoring payments to the seller. This ensures that payment terms defined within the contract are met and that the seller's compensation is linked to seller progress as defined in the contract.

One of the principal concerns when making payments to suppliers is that there is a close relationship of payments made to the work accomplished. When you administer procurements, you are required to review and document how well a seller is performing or has performed based on the contract and establish corrective actions when needed.

This performance review may be used as a measure of the seller's competency for performing similar work on future projects. Similar evaluations are also carried out when it is necessary to confirm that a seller is not meeting the seller's contractual obligations and when the buyer contemplates corrective action.

Administering procurements includes managing any early terminations of the contracted work in accordance with the termination clause of the contract. Some reasons for early termination may include termination for cause, convenience, or default.

Contracts may be amended at any time prior to contract closure by mutual consent, in accordance with the change control terms of the contract. Such amendments may not always be equally beneficial to both the seller and the buyer.

Close Project or Phase

Two things are required to close a project:

1. Close the project or phase.
2. Close procurements.

When you close the project or phase, you finalize all activities across all of the project management process groups to formally complete the project or phase. When closing the project, the project manager will review all prior information from the previous phase closures to ensure that all project work is complete and that the project has met its objectives.

Since project scope is measured against the project management plan, as project manager you will review that document to ensure completion before considering the project closed.

Characteristics Common to All Projects During the Closing Process

The probability of completing the project is highest during this process and risk is lowest. Stakeholders have the least amount of influence during the closing processes, while project managers have the greatest amount of influence. Costs are significantly lower during this process because the majority of the project work and spending has already occurred.

Document the Reasons for Action Taken If the Project Is Terminated Before Completion

In the event that the project is terminated before completion, you should document the reasons for the action taken. This includes all of the activities necessary for administrative closure of the project or phase, including step-by-step methods that address:

- Actions and activities necessary to satisfy completion or exit criteria for the phase or project.
- Actions or activities necessary to transfer the project's products, services, or results to the next phase or to production or operations.
- Activities needed to collect project or phase records, audit project success or failure, gather lessons learned, and archive project information for future use by the organization.

Project Endings

Projects come to an end for several reasons:

- They are successfully completed.
- They are cancelled or killed prior to completion.

- They evolve into ongoing operations and no longer exist as projects.

Four Formal Types of Project Endings

1. Addition.
2. Starvation.
3. Integration.
4. Extinction.

Addition

Projects that evolve into ongoing operations are considered projects that end because of addition. In other words, they become an ongoing business unit. When a project becomes an ongoing operation, it is no longer a project.

Starvation

When resources are cut off from the project or are no longer provided to the project, it is starved prior to completing all the requirements. Resource starving may include cutting back or withholding human resources, equipment and supplies, or money. Some reasons for starvation are:

- Other projects come about and take precedence over the current project, thereby cutting the funding or resources for your project.
- The customer curtails the order.
- The project budget is reduced.
- A key resource quits.

Integration

Integration occurs when the resources of the project—people, equipment, property, and supplies—are distributed to other areas in the organization or are assigned to other projects.

Extinction

This is the best kind of project end because extinction means that the project has been completed and accepted by the stakeholders. As such, it no longer exists because it had a definite ending date, the goals of the project were achieved, and the project was closed out.

Key Activity in Project Closeout

The key activity that the closed project or phase process is concerned with is gathering project records and disseminating information to formalize acceptance of the product, service, or result, as well as to perform project closure. You should review the project documents to make sure that they are up-to-date. For example, perhaps some scope change requests were implemented that changed some characteristics of the final product. The project information that is collected during this process should reflect the characteristics and specifications of the final product.

You may need to update some resource assignments. Some team members will have come and gone over the course of the project. Double-check to see that the resources and their roles and responsibilities are noted.

Once the project outcome is documented, you will request formal acceptance from the stakeholders or the customers. The stakeholders or the customers are also interested in knowing whether the product or service of the project meets the goals that the project set out to accomplish. If the documentation is up-to-date, you have the project results at hand to share with them.

The closed project or phase process is also concerned with analyzing the project management processes to determine their effectiveness and to document lessons learned concerning the project processes. Another key function of the closed project or phase process is to archive all project documents for historical reference. The closed project or phase belongs to the integration management knowledge area, because this process touches so many areas of the project.

Results of Closing the Project or Phase

The two results of closing a project or phase include:

1. Final product, service, or result transition.
2. Organizational process assets update.

Final Product, Service, or Result Transition

This refers to the transition of the final product, service, or result that the project was authorized to produce. In the case of phase closure, final product, service, or result transition refers to the intermediate product, service, or result of that phase. Otherwise, final product, service, or result transition refers to the acceptance of the final product, service, or result and the turning over of the product to the organization.

This usually requires a final sign-off or receipt indicating acceptance of the project. Formal acceptance includes distributing notice of the acceptance of the product or service of the project by the stakeholders, customer, or project sponsor. Final sign-off should be required, indicating that those signing accept the product of the project.

Organizational Processes

The organizational processes that are updated as a result of the closed project or closed phase process include, but are not limited to:

Project Files

Examples of documentation resulting from the project's activities include project management plan, scope, cost, schedule and project calendars, risk registers, change management documentation, planned risk response actions, and risk impact.

Project or Phase Closure Documents

Project or phase closure documents consist of formal documentation that include completion of the project or phase and the transfer of the completed project or phase deliverables to others, such as an operations group or to the next phase.

During project closure, as project manager you should review prior phase documentation, customer acceptance documentation from the verify scope process, and the contract (if applicable). This is done to ensure that all project requirements are complete prior to finalizing project closure. If the project was terminated prior to completion, the formal documentation indicates why the project was terminated and formalizes the procedures for the transfer of the finished and unfinished deliverables of the cancelled project to others.

Historical Information

You should ensure that historical information and lessons learned information are transferred to the lessons learned knowledge base for use by future projects or phases. This may include information on issues and risks, as well as techniques that worked well, that may be applied to future projects.

Key Points to Remember

- Administering procurements is the process of monitoring your vendor's performance and ensuring that all the requirements of the contracts are met.
- Both the buyer and the seller must administer the procurement contract for similar reasons. Each ensures that both parties meet their contractual obligations and that their own legal rights are protected.
- The purpose of administering procurements ensures that the seller's performance meets procurement requirements and

that the buyer performs according to the terms of the legal contract.

- Administering procurements has a financial management component that involves monitoring payments to the seller.
- When you administer procurements, you are required to review and document how well a seller is performing or has performed based on the contract and establish corrective actions when needed.
- Administering procurements also includes managing any early termination of the contracted work in accordance with the termination clause of the contract.
- Two things required to close a project are to close the project or phase and to close procurements.
- When you close a project or phase, you finalize all activities across all of the project management process groups to formally complete the project or phase.
- The probability of completing the project is highest during the project-closing process and the risk is lowest.
- You should document the reasons for action taken in the event that the project is terminated before completion.
- Projects come to an end because they are successfully completed, they are cancelled or killed before completion, or they evolve into ongoing operations and no longer exist as projects.
- The four formal types of project endings are addition, starvation, integration, and extinction.
- The key activity that the closed project or phase process is concerned with is gathering project records and disseminating information to formally accept the product, service, or result, as well as to perform project closure.
- Once the project outcome is documented, you will request formal acceptance from the stakeholders or the customers.
- The two results of closing a project or phase include final product, service, or result transition and updating the organizational process assets.
- During project closure, the project manager should review prior phase documentation, customer acceptance documentation from the verify scope process, and the contract (if applicable).

This is done to ensure that all project requirements are completed prior to finalizing project closure.

Discussion Questions

1. Why should both the buyer and the seller administer the procurement contract?
2. What is the purpose of administering procurements?
3. What does the financial aspect of administering procurements entail?
4. What should be a principal concern when making payments to suppliers?
5. When can contracts be amended in a project?
6. What are two things required to close a project?
7. What does closing a project or phase entail?
8. What are some characteristics common to all projects during the closing process?
9. What should you do in the event that the project is terminated before completion?
10. Why do projects come to an end?
11. What are four formal types of project endings?
12. What is the key activity that the close project or phase is concerned with?
13. What are the two results of closing a project or phase?
14. What must the project manager do during the project closure process?

Debrief Questions

1. What are the key learning points?
2. What information was new to you?
3. Which concepts will you apply in the future? When?
4. What challenges do you anticipate that may limit your ability to apply the concepts?
5. What needs to be in place to overcome these challenges?
6. Who would you recommend these concepts to and why?

Activity

The following is an activity that may be completed in project teams:

1. Answer the discussion questions.
2. Answer the debrief questions.

About the Author

Dorcas M. T. Cox, PMP

Dorcas is a project manager and the founder of Project Management Solutions Limited, a successful human resources development and project management consulting company. She has worked for multinational corporations and as an adjunct instructor for several academic institutions including The College of The Bahamas. More recently, she has worked at The Bahamas Institute of Financial Services (BIFS), where she teaches a course designed to prepare students to sit and pass the Project Management Professional (PMP) exam or the Certified Associate in Project Management (CAPM) exam Dorcas has studied, lived, and worked in North America and Canada and received her Project Management Professional (PMP) distinction from the Project Management Institute.

Dorcas has consulted with multinational clients on how to best manage employees and projects. Her expert direction is applicable to everyone, from recent graduates looking to make themselves more marketable for that first job, to high-ranking executives wanting to further hone their expertise. Dorcas has authored several books, including *Project Management Skills for Instructional Designers* and its corresponding workbook and *Passing the PMP Exam Learner Guide*.

Resources

Project Management Institute. *A Guide to the Project Management Body of Knowledge: PMBOK Guide*, 4th ed. Project Management Institute, 2008.

www.ingramcontent.com/pod-product-compliance
Lightning Source LLC
Chambersburg PA
CBHW032023170526
45157CB00002B/833